STANLEY BREEDEN

AUSTRALIAN WORLD HERITAGE TROPICAL
RAINFOREST
A JOURNEY OF DISCOVERY

Steve Parish
PUBLISHING

CONTENTS

« Buttresses of a Rose Alder tree

ACKNOWLEDGEMENTS

Flowers of a Wheel-of-fire tree

It has taken nearly two years to do the photography, gather the information and write the text for this book. It has been a great adventure. The adventure was made all the more memorable by the people who, through their encouragement, enthusiasm, discussions, and generously giving of their knowledge, enriched my experiences and shed light on many of the rainforest's fascinating mysteries and enigmas. The thanks expressed below are an inadequate measure of my appreciation.

I am especially grateful to Bill and Wendy Cooper for their support. In many ways, through our discussions and excursions into the forest, they shared the adventure. Wendy Cooper undertook the complex task of identifying the plants that appear in this volume. I thank Marion Buchanan for her company on numerous field trips. I am indebted to many people in helping to find special places and species to photograph — the Hasenpusch family for innumerable insects, Bruce Gray for orchids, Yvonne Cunningham for trees and places near Innisfail, Rob and Ruth Whiston for freshwater fishes, Bill Bayne for showing me Lake Barrine at its very best, Margit Cianelli for Lumholtz's Tree-kangaroo and Mike and Segang McGough for getting me to Hope Island under such special circumstances. I also wish to thank Andrew Dennis for sharing his knowledge, the many discussions and the use of his beautiful and unique photographs of the white phase of the Lemuroid Ringtail Possum and also those of the summit of Mount Bartle Frere; Geoff Monteith of the Queensland Museum, not only for identifying many insects but also his infectious passion for the rainforest and all its natural inhabitants; Mike Graham for enlightening me on the region's geology; Graeme Newell for the use of his photographs of the devastation in part of his tree-kangaroo study site; Belinda Wright for the use of a score of her beautiful pictures; Steve Parish for the aerial photograph of Hinchinbrook Island; and Ian Morris for his picture of the Spotted-tailed Quoll.

I am most grateful to Dr David Christophel for illuminating what is to me the most fascinating of all the rainforest stories — their long and continuous history in this corner of Australia. I also appreciate the work by Cath Jones in gathering most of the material on the national parks, state forests and other reserves. I am indebted to Elva Castino who once again worked her magic on my handwritten pages and turned them into a legible and pleasing-looking manuscript. I extend a special thanks to Steve and Jan Parish who, through their enthusiasm and support, brought this project to fruition.

Stanley Breeden
Topaz, May 1999

INTRODUCTION

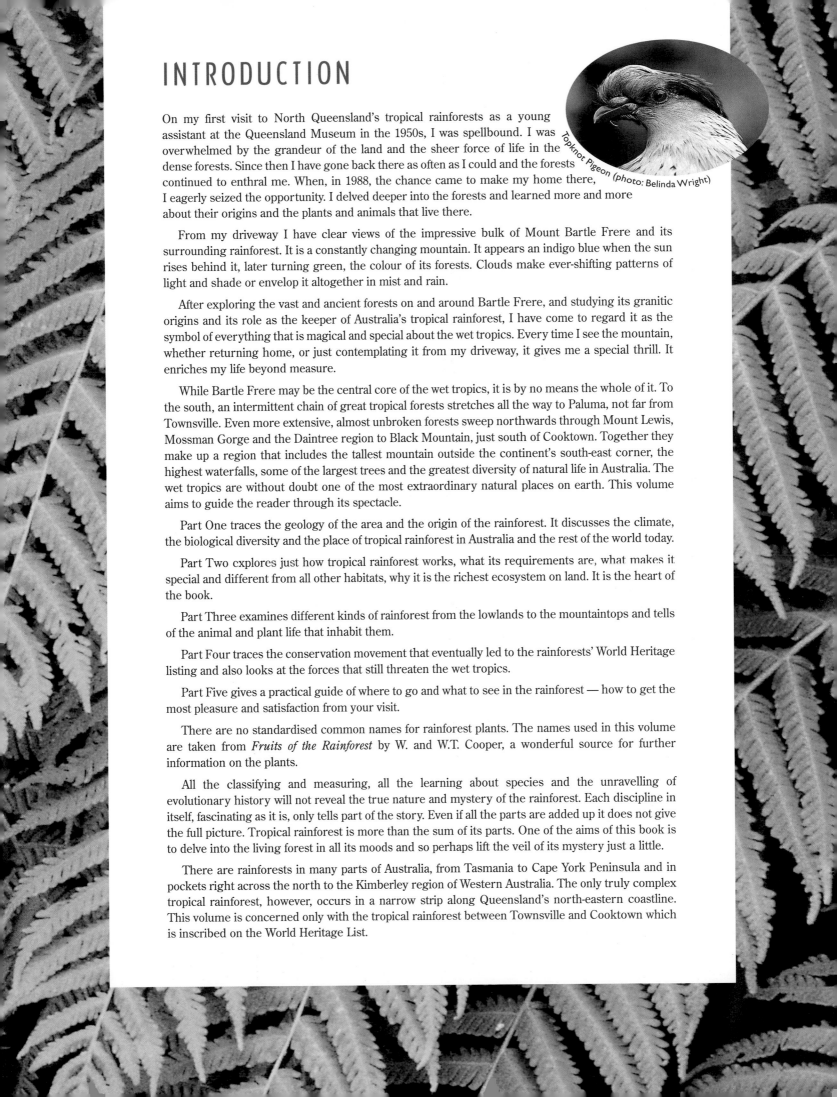

Topknot Pigeon (photo: Belinda Wright)

On my first visit to North Queensland's tropical rainforests as a young assistant at the Queensland Museum in the 1950s, I was spellbound. I was overwhelmed by the grandeur of the land and the sheer force of life in the dense forests. Since then I have gone back there as often as I could and the forests continued to enthral me. When, in 1988, the chance came to make my home there, I eagerly seized the opportunity. I delved deeper into the forests and learned more and more about their origins and the plants and animals that live there.

From my driveway I have clear views of the impressive bulk of Mount Bartle Frere and its surrounding rainforest. It is a constantly changing mountain. It appears an indigo blue when the sun rises behind it, later turning green, the colour of its forests. Clouds make ever-shifting patterns of light and shade or envelop it altogether in mist and rain.

After exploring the vast and ancient forests on and around Bartle Frere, and studying its granitic origins and its role as the keeper of Australia's tropical rainforest, I have come to regard it as the symbol of everything that is magical and special about the wet tropics. Every time I see the mountain, whether returning home, or just contemplating it from my driveway, it gives me a special thrill. It enriches my life beyond measure.

While Bartle Frere may be the central core of the wet tropics, it is by no means the whole of it. To the south, an intermittent chain of great tropical forests stretches all the way to Paluma, not far from Townsville. Even more extensive, almost unbroken forests sweep northwards through Mount Lewis, Mossman Gorge and the Daintree region to Black Mountain, just south of Cooktown. Together they make up a region that includes the tallest mountain outside the continent's south-east corner, the highest waterfalls, some of the largest trees and the greatest diversity of natural life in Australia. The wet tropics are without doubt one of the most extraordinary natural places on earth. This volume aims to guide the reader through its spectacle.

Part One traces the geology of the area and the origin of the rainforest. It discusses the climate, the biological diversity and the place of tropical rainforest in Australia and the rest of the world today.

Part Two explores just how tropical rainforest works, what its requirements are, what makes it special and different from all other habitats, why it is the richest ecosystem on land. It is the heart of the book.

Part Three examines different kinds of rainforest from the lowlands to the mountaintops and tells of the animal and plant life that inhabit them.

Part Four traces the conservation movement that eventually led to the rainforests' World Heritage listing and also looks at the forces that still threaten the wet tropics.

Part Five gives a practical guide of where to go and what to see in the rainforest — how to get the most pleasure and satisfaction from your visit.

There are no standardised common names for rainforest plants. The names used in this volume are taken from *Fruits of the Rainforest* by W. and W.T. Cooper, a wonderful source for further information on the plants.

All the classifying and measuring, all the learning about species and the unravelling of evolutionary history will not reveal the true nature and mystery of the rainforest. Each discipline in itself, fascinating as it is, only tells part of the story. Even if all the parts are added up it does not give the full picture. Tropical rainforest is more than the sum of its parts. One of the aims of this book is to delve into the living forest in all its moods and so perhaps lift the veil of its mystery just a little.

There are rainforests in many parts of Australia, from Tasmania to Cape York Peninsula and in pockets right across the north to the Kimberley region of Western Australia. The only truly complex tropical rainforest, however, occurs in a narrow strip along Queensland's north-eastern coastline. This volume is concerned only with the tropical rainforest between Townsville and Cooktown which is inscribed on the World Heritage List.

Male Dwarf Tree Frog calling

Just a few kilometres from the Coral Sea coast in tropical north Queensland stands Mount Bartle Frere. At 1622 metres, it is Australia's tallest mountain outside the high country of the south-east of the continent. For millions of years the mountain has captured moisture brought in by incessant trade winds and monsoonal convergences. To this day, the highest annual rainfall and the most copious downpours in Australia fall on and around this gigantic outcrop of granite. No rainfall has been measured on the mountain itself, but the neighbouring peak of Mount Bellenden Ker, which is 1560 metres high, receives an annual rainfall of more than 9000 mm. In one 24-hour period in 1979 it was deluged by 1140 mm of rain. A collaboration of tropical warmth, moisture-laden winds, and mountains that transform clouds into mist and rain, has created complex rainforest and wild, spectacular scenery unrivalled in Australia.

On those mountains, there have been rainforests of flowering plants as long as these have existed on earth: about 100 million years. Even when the surrounding country became cooler and drier during ice ages and could sustain only open woodlands, as recently as 15 000 to 10 000 years ago, tropical rainforest remained in these massifs' recesses. Once heavy rains returned, the rainforests re-colonised the surrounding land. The forests are now

QUEENSLAND'S WET TROPICS

"It is easy to specify the individual objects of admiration in those grand scenes; but it is not possible to give an adequate idea of the higher feelings of wonder, astonishment, and devotion, which fill and elevate the mind."

CHARLES DARWIN ON A BRAZILIAN RAINFOREST
HE VISITED ON 18 APRIL 1832

expanding again. They are luxuriant places where forests grow within forests, their trees woven together by gigantic lianes, where ferns and mosses smother streamside boulders. They are places of brilliantly-coloured flowers and fruits, of birds of paradise and cassowaries, of Green Possums and kangaroos that climb trees, of enormous pythons and dazzling butterflies, of myriad frogs and an ever-shifting, often elusive beauty.

Mounts Bartle Frere and Bellenden Ker form the core, the very heart of the wet tropics. Other, lower mountain ranges to the south and the north also combine with the winds and clouds to bring high, year-round rainfall. Between them they roll out a narrow band of rainforest along the Coral Sea coast — a ribbon of intense green along the edge of a great brown continent. Even though this stretch of forest makes up less than one-thousandth of Australia's land surface, it is home to the greatest variety of plants and animals. It is also all that remains of the original source of Australia's other forests and woodlands.

Zodiac Moth

Fan Palm frond

Female cassowary

White-tailed Kingfisher

« Trees silhouetted against Mount Bartle Frere

JOURNEY ALONG THE RIBBON OF GREEN

Blue Quandong tree in Paluma rainforest

« Open forest adjoining the rainforest at Paluma

When you approach the ribbon of green that makes up the World Heritage tropical rainforest from the south, it first appears on the Paluma Range, just north of Townsville. It comes to a full stop at Black Mountain, not far south of Cooktown, about 450 km further along the coast.

You reach Paluma's cool, dark green hills after travelling countless kilometres through sparse woodlands and forests (where these have not been replaced by farmlands), whose leaves have a blue-green foliage. The understorey is mostly brown and yellowed grasses.

Imagine that your rainforest journey begins at Witt's Lookout on the crest of the Paluma Range. You stand on exposed granite rocks surrounded by eucalypt, turpentine, banksia, box, and casuarina trees. The undergrowth consists of tea trees, bottle brushes with a few bright red flowers, and grass trees.

Paluma's rainforest-covered hills; the southern gateway to the wet tropics.

Banksias, turpentines, casuarinas and grass trees at Witt's Lookout

It is a classic Australian forest you might see anywhere in drier areas along the east coast.

To the north you see towering granite outcrops, but to the east and south, directly below you, there are slopes covered in unbroken, variegated, bright green forests. The canopy is closed so you can see nothing of grasses or other understorey plants. There is no sign of any of the eucalypts, turpentines or casuarinas. Swirls of mist rise up the valley and occasionally envelop you — a soft damp touch on your face. In the distance the rising sun glints on the Coral Sea.

Witt's Lookout could be considered the gateway to the tropical rainforest, for as you walk down the track, you suddenly leave the ubiquitous open forest behind, and enter a completely different world. It is immediately darker and greener. There is a great exuberance of plant growth and birdsong. The trunks of most trees have thin, smooth bark, not rough and furrowed. Many have elegantly curved buttresses. No two trees seem to be of the same species. Mosses and ferns, some in giant clumps, grow on their limbs and on the boulders. Huge woody lianes loop and claw their way to the canopy. The forest floor is devoid of grass or bracken. A sometimes deep layer of damp, brown leaf-litter softens your footfall. Tender-leafed seedlings and shrubs struggle to survive in the low light. You have entered the realm of flowering plants, their greatest expression on earth. They are also ancient forests where, as explained later, the ancestors of the classic Australian trees, the eucalypts, banksias and so on, still live. Not that the rainforest reaches its zenith here. Because Paluma is nearly 900 m in altitude, these are not the most luxuriant or diverse forests: they are on the lowlands and uplands to the north.

THE CARDWELL RANGE

Hinchinbrook Island (photo: Steve Parish)

After you descend from Paluma, this greater luxuriance and variety is at first not at all apparent. As you travel north you pass through paperbark swamps, eucalypt woodlands and interminable fields of sugar cane. Even the slopes of the Paluma and Seaview Ranges have the paler colours of open woodland. Only on the highest points and fingering down the occasional stream bed will you see the dark green of rainforest. Seaview Range bends inland. It is barely visible in the distance as you drive through more and more cane fields.

Just north of Ingham there is a sudden change. Low foothills covered in rainforest run down from the Cardwell Range and cross the road. From a vantage point there are wide and spectacular views of Hinchinbrook Island — Australia's largest island national park and much of it rainforest wilderness. It is separated from the mainland by a narrow channel that meanders through bright green mangrove forests. There are several peaks over 900 m high on the island: the highest, Mount Bowen, is 1121 m tall.

After crossing these foothills, rainforest once more retreats to the hilltops. It is not until you approach Tully that you feel you have reached the heartland of the wet tropics. Surrounded by rainforest-covered hills, you become aware that all the lowlands to the north and east were once covered in rainforest. You travel through remnant patches. Clumps of tall palms and rugged old milky pines, figs or other trees stand as reminders in seas of grass and cane. Strips of rainforest run along some creeks and rivers. At Innisfail the Palmerston Highway heads westward to the Atherton Tableland and passes through some of the few unlogged forests, now part of Wooroonooran National Park.

Alexandra Palm and other trees against misty mountains near Tully

« Mountains near Tully

WOOROONOORAN NATIONAL PARK

Continuing north from Innisfail, the granite massifs of Mounts Bartle Frere and Bellenden Ker, also part of Wooroonooran National Park, loom larger and larger. The highway skirts along their rainforest-covered foothills that rise steeply to the usually misty summits. At last you feel the wild tropicalness of the region. The mountains create their own climate with ever-shifting patterns of towering white clouds, low blankets of almost black clouds, sudden rain, and equally abrupt and unpredictable periods of sunshine.

Flowers of Pink Silky Oak

You might decide to drive towards the mountains at Josephine Falls or The Boulders. You will soon be close enough to smell the forests and see individual trees, not just an inchoate mass of green. There will be glimpses of waterfalls. Finally, deep in the forest, you will see fast-flowing streams of clear water, wide pools, huge tumbles of granite boulders and water-sculpted rock outcrops. You will suddenly be immersed in the forest — vines, buttressed trees, a flash of a brilliant butterfly or bird, a tree covered in bright red flowers, blue or yellow fruits strewn over the brown leaf-litter, sweet songs of birds or their strange booming and bubbling calls. A patch of sun may illuminate the gloss on a snake's skin.

All the way to Cairns, on both sides of the highway there are rainforest-covered ranges. The city's special charm is that it is surrounded by green hills.

Mount Bartle Frere — part of Wooroonooran National Park

Josephine Falls

Amethyst Python (photo: Belinda Wright)

Mount Bartle Frere at sunrise

Mount Bartle Frere in late afternoon

MOSSMAN

View over Wangetti Beach along the Cook Highway

Continuing northwards along the Cook Highway, one of the country's most spectacular routes, you are once again among paperbarks and eucalypts. The road winds along a narrow strip between the sea and the steep slopes of the MacAlister Range. Here and there grow scrubby rainforests — leaning away from the wind. They are not luxuriant, tall growths; it is too windy and too dry for that.

At Yule Point, a short distance south of the turn-off to Port Douglas, there is a northward view along mangroves and sandy beaches towards the mountains of the Daintree region. Tall peaks, nearly always with clouds around their summits, give promise of another great wilderness area of uninterrupted rainforest. Close at hand, at Yule Point, it is much drier and there is, in fact, a narrow corridor without rainforest — the first such break since the Seaview Range.

In Mossman Gorge

Well before you reach Mossman you will have crossed this corridor. Once again hills and mountains are high enough and close enough to the sea to pull rain out of the moisture-laden trade winds. At Mossman Gorge the river rushes and tumbles out of the green hills over and through the boulders that choke its course. In clear pools a colourful fish leaps at low-flying insects. Almost constant low cloud and moisture from the turbulent river succour the dense gardens of aerial plants — lichens, mosses, ferns and orchids — that festoon the trees and enwrap the boulders. Hills surround a bowl of low country where huge trees with intricately formed and elegantly curved buttresses grow sheltered from the fierce, tree-toppling winds of cyclones.

Ferns and other epiphytes on a riverside tree in Mossman Gorge

« A bouldery beach between Mossman and Cairns

DAINTREE

View of the Daintree region from Yule Point

Cyclone-damaged rainforest smothered in vines, Daintree National Park

Rainforest sweeps from the hills to the beach at Emmagen Creek in Daintree National Park

North of Mossman the road skirts the sea again. Rainforest-covered hills are visible in the west, if the clouds are not too low and the sugar cane is not too tall.

When you cross the Daintree River you enter a veritable feast of forests — paperbarks, wattles, mangroves at first, then fan palms, and at last the most luxuriant forests of all: the broad-leafed lowland rainforest. It once grew along the coast all the way to Cardwell.

Daintree National Park runs as a narrow strip along the coast from the Daintree River to the Bloomfield River. As well as its varied rainforests, the park's glory is its beaches, or, more specifically, beaches backed by tall mountains. Rainforests sweep down from their misty heights right to the fringe of golden sand arcing between rocky headlands.

Cape Tribulation and its mountainous surrounds form another core area of tropical rainforest. Rainfall is as high as at the Bartle Frere–Bellenden Ker complex and the forests here are as diverse.

Those directly facing the sea, however, often have a ravaged look about them. This is a legacy of the cyclones that periodically spiral in across the Coral Sea bringing winds of over 100 km/h whose destructive power is enormous. When they reach land, they snap and uproot trees and strip the entire forest of leaves.

The first species to recover after such devastation are the vigorous climbing plants, opportunists that respond swiftly to the increased sunlight. Whole forests on this coast are smothered by them, evidence of a severe cyclone in the last 50 years or so.

BLACK MOUNTAIN

Gap Creek in Cedar Bay National Park

North of Cape Tribulation rainfall decreases rapidly. Ancient, shaggy paperbark trees mix with fan palms and other rainforest trees in low-lying swamps. On the ridges, more and more wattles infiltrate the rainforest, and, by the time you reach the north bank of the Bloomfield River, pockets of eucalypts and casuarinas have grown into forests of their own, with only a few rainforest species among them.

At Cedar Bay National Park steep hills covered in forests of an infinite variety of shades of green, trimmed and layered by the tradewinds, rise on both sides of the road. The tall plumes of Alexandra Palms project above the canopy: their flexible stems bend in the wind; they are not snapped by it. Gap Creek runs parallel to the road for many kilometres. Cool water shaded by wide, spreading trees burbles gently from one rock pool to another. Fish nibble at fallen leaves and flowers and snap up any insects that accidentally blunder into the water. Frogs, some bright green, others the colour of pale stones, hide among mossy boulders. The songs of Black Butcherbirds and the booming of amorous Pied Imperial-Pigeons reverberate down the slopes.

Rainforest continues for some distance further along the coast, but the road bends slightly westwards, where the rain is considerably less. Immediately rainforest is dominated first by wattles then by paperbarks, until it is eventually overtaken completely by eucalypts, casuarinas, grass trees and other drought-tolerant species. The country once again looks as it did at Paluma.

« Black Mountain

On the northward-sweeping hills, rain-forests persist until they end abruptly at a spectacular agglomeration of enormous black rocks. Rocks larger than houses are haphazardly piled into a range of mountains. The black is a covering of lichen growing on granite – which itself is pale grey in colour. Caves and passages run in and out among the blocks of stone creating a habitat for specialist animals. Rock wallabies live in the caverns by day and come out to graze and browse on the surrounding vegetation at night. Swiftlets glue their flimsy nests on cave walls with their saliva. Of the lizards and frogs that hunt for insects among the rocks, three species are found only here at Black Mountain.

Tentacles of rainforest run into the mountain's southern valleys but do not emerge on the northern side. A few fig trees, whose roots reach down to the water table, have taken hold here and there, otherwise the mountain is bare.

The complex World Heritage tropical rainforest comes to an end at Black Mountain. There are a few small pockets in hidden valleys immediately to the north but these are of a less complex type. On Cape York Peninsula there are areas of extensive rainforest, but these are different in character and are not World Heritage listed.

Framed by immense granite rocks and hardy dry-country trees, the end of the complex tropical rainforests is as dramatic as their beginning.

Ringtailed Geckos live among Black Mountain's rocks.

The giant blocks of granite of Black Mountain are really pale grey. They are covered with black lichen.

Black Mountain

THE COAST

Mangrove forest

In a journey from east to west across the wet tropics you will find that the yearly average rainfall drops off sharply. At its widest, the rainforest spans about 80 km, from Mourilyan Harbour to Tully Falls. It is only a few kilometres wide near Julatten, north of Cairns.

On the eastern boundary, in the wide river and creek estuaries, mangroves grow into dense forests. The extensive sandy and pebbly beaches are lined by special rainforests mixed with casuarinas, paperbarks and coconut palms. Beyond the beaches, ridges of sand impound long strips of swamp. Their waterlogged, infertile soils support little rainforest. Mostly they contain paperbarks and pandans, some casuarinas and just a few special rainforest trees such as the Red Beech and the calophyllum. More extensive seasonal marshes beyond the coastal fringe are the home of the fascinating and mysterious palm forests.

Sometimes gradually, sometimes abruptly, the swamplands give way to lowland rainforest — the most varied and luxuriant type of all. There are few places where these remain.

Lowland rainforest along the coast

« Mangroves

Weeping Paperbark trees growing in a swamp behind the beach

THE TABLELANDS

Wallicher Falls in the Palmerston Section of Wooroonooran National Park

When travelling from the coast to the Atherton Tableland and beyond to the mountain ranges on their western edge, it is necessary to climb the escarpment that runs virtually the full length of the wet tropics. High rainfall and the resulting dense rainforest, together with deep ravines and waterfalls, create wild landscapes. The most accessible of these are in the Palmerston section of Wooroonooran National Park, just south of Mount Bartle Frere, right beside the Palmerston Highway that ascends to the Atherton Tableland.

Even though they are in the shadow of the tall mountains, the Tablelands themselves still receive high rainfall. They were once covered with rainforest. Because they are sheltered from the destructive force of cyclones, and are covered in deep, red, volcanic soils, the tallest trees of the greatest girth grow on these Tablelands. Only tiny remnants of these types of forest remain, at Lakes Eacham and Barrine, at Malanda Falls, and a few other places.

Unlogged rainforest in the Palmerston Section of Wooroonooran

« A giant Stockwellia tree on the Atherton Tableland

The hills of the Great Dividing Range rise on the Tablelands' western edge. These colder, more wind-battered altitudes result in less complex forests. They are also the last bastion of the rainforest, for, on the crest of the Divide where it slopes gently into the western plains, rainfall drops off abruptly. The change from rainforest into eucalypt woodland is different here from that at the southern and northern limits. Truly gigantic flooded gums, brush boxes and turpentine trees rise out of a rainforest understorey.

Moving westward, the rainforest species become fewer and fewer, being replaced by casuarina, cypress pines, wattles and different species of eucalypt. Soon it is so dry that only bloodwoods, ironbarks, stringy-barks and a few other trees grow in a grassy understorey. The change from complex rainforest to grass and eucalypts can take place in just a few hundred metres. It is all the result of decreasing rainfall. At Innisfail on the coast, for example, the annual average rainfall is 3550 mm, while at Herberton, 60

km to the west, it is only 1100 mm.

The east-west section divides the rainforest into three broad categories — lowlands along the coast, uplands on the tablelands, and those on the mountain tops. Each division has its own special forest types, plants and animals, and its own special feel and ambience.

This narrow strip of rainforest, the ribbon of green, is the result of special weather conditions. But what exactly are these?

Rainforest grades into eucalypt forest. Smooth, white Rose Gums, on the right, and turpentines, Cypress Pines and casuarinas, on the left, grow in a gully filled with gingers and rainforest shrubs.

CLIMATE AND SEASONS

Drizzly rain on the Atherton Tableland

The tropical climate does not readily fit into the classic four-season pattern. It could be said that there is a wet season and a drier one. But it is more subtle than that. There are three wet seasons and two that are drier. The first wet season begins in mid-November and brings a succession of often violent thunderstorms. The days are hot, the hottest of the year. When the wind is from the west, temperatures can reach close to 40°C. This is followed by the true monsoon, when blankets of clouds roll in from the north and north-west and bring days and days of heavy rain. Creeks and rivers flood. The monsoon can start any time from the end of December, but usually does not arrive till January or even early February. It departs again in early April. February and March are the months of heaviest rainfall.

Rain dripping from the leaves of a Pink Ash

In April the third wet season begins. From then until early June there are weeks on end of mist and light drizzly rain, especially on the tablelands. In conventional, temperate climate terms April is autumn; in the wet tropics it is a time when many of the trees and vines put on new leaf. Quite a few are in flower.

Superimposed on these wet seasons is a force of occasional but catastrophic violence. Tropical cyclones can whirl in from the Coral Sea any time between November and May. They are completely capricious and can strike anywhere along the coast. However, once they cross the coastline their force is dissipated quickly and their full destructive power rarely reaches beyond the coastal fringe.

On average, two cyclones approach the wet tropics each season. Most spin by, well out to sea, leaving only flood rain as a legacy of their passage. The most recent severe cyclone to invade the wet tropics was Cyclone Winifred. It crossed the coastline, just south of Innisfail, in the early evening of 1 February 1986. The lowland rain-forests between the Russell and Tully Rivers were buffeted by gales gusting up to 176 km/h. Almost all the forests in the area — to a distance of 50 km inland — were stripped of their leaves. Many tall trees had their crowns and large limbs torn off. Others had their trunks snapped or were uprooted. Vines and clumps of epiphytic ferns were ripped out of the tree tops and smashed to the ground. The next morning it appeared as though not a tree had been left standing. The hillsides were no longer green, but brown. Along the beach, the wind had even peeled the bark off the paperbark trees, giving them an eerie, naked and pink appearance.

« Clouds roll in over Mount Bartle Frere.

So much debris accumulated that the forests became impenetrable. Animal life was also severely affected, especially the birds. Both insect-eaters and fruit-eaters had difficulty gathering food. Many perished.

The severe damage covered an area up to 70 000 hectares. Another area of roughly the same size had lesser damage. Other severe cyclones hit the coast between Innisfail and Cairns in 1918 and 1956. Their effects, as well as those of Cyclone Winifred, can still be seen in coastal forests. While they recover from the catastrophes to a degree, the forests remain permanently scarred because of the inescapable frequency of the cyclones. They become cyclone scrubs — forests without really gigantic trees, choked with vines.

Five Mile Creek in a wet season flood

Five Mile Creek during the dry season

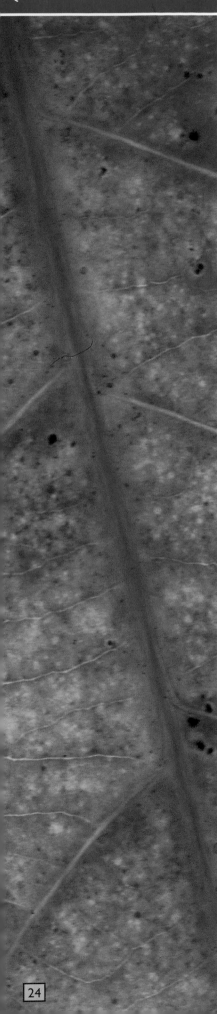

Although it may rain one or even two weeks at a time, there are always sunny breaks. March and April are the months with most rainy days, but, on average, these months have eight rainless days each in even the wettest places. These are special days, ones to revel in the forest's freshness, in the new growth and the animals' seeming joy at the relief from wet weather. But even on days of drizzle the special character and feel of the forest are enjoyable. It is a time when the forest seems at its most dynamic, when it is truly *rain*forest.

The drier seasons — there is no completely dry one — are comparatively brief, lasting from about mid-June to mid-November. During June, July and early August there are lengthy periods when the skies are clear and there is very little wind. Mount Bartle Frere and the other peaks then appear etched against the sky. The days are balmy. The night sky fairly crackles with stars. Early mornings are crisp and on one or two days frost dresses the grass in low-lying areas of the tablelands in white. Frost, however, never invades the forest.

In September, the weather slowly warms.

New leaves on a Hard Alder

Birdsong swells in volume and variety. Nesting begins and continues into January for most species. You might think this warm, dry season is spring, but then this is the season when there is the greatest leaf fall. Nearly all the trees are evergreen, of course, and do not shed all their leaves. But enough do fall at this time of year to make the forest noticeably lighter.

However, the wet tropics are far enough from the equator to have faint traces of the temperate climate pattern. They are in the tropics, but not in the equatorial zone. Days are longer in summer than in winter. The winter sun is lower in the sky, which means that steep slopes facing the south and deep gullies receive little or no sunshine for several months. So even though there are wet times and dry times, there are also traces of summer and winter, spring and autumn.

While climate is the most important factor in determining whether rainforests can thrive, just how well they do, how complex they are, also depend on the types of soils and the topography. To appreciate these we have to look at the underlying rocks and the forces that shaped them.

Flowers of a Johnstone River Satinash

« The dying leaf of a Bleeding Heart tree

Male Satin Bowerbirds build their bowers in spring.

FORMATION OF THE ROCKS

A waterfall at Crystal Cascades tumbles over Hodgkinson Formation rocks.

In the late Silurian Period, about 420 million years ago, the area between what is now Townsville and Cooktown was beneath the sea. It was part of the Hodgkinson Basin, which was thousands of metres deep. The edge of the Australian continent was then more than 100 km further west, along a line roughly between Palmerville and Chillagoe.

During the next 80 million years, vast quantities of sediments, from coarse gravel to fine mud, were eroded from the landmass and deposited in the basin's depths by the river systems. Sediments 10 000 m thick, more than three times the height of the highest mountain in Australia today, were laid down. The weight of these sediments compacted them into rocks — from fine-grained mudstone and shale to coarse sandstone and even conglomerate. The lava of submarine volcanoes turned into basalt and added to the accumulation of rock. All the layers of rock together became known as the Hodgkinson Formation.

The long, slow filling in of the basin came to an end about 360 million years ago. Plates within the earth's crust then moved against each other causing great upheavals. As the continental land mass ground inexorably eastward and upwards, against the sediments and basalt of the Hodgkinson Formation, its layers crumpled, buckled and folded into steep-sided mountains. Being compressed, they rose up and up and finally emerged from the sea. Mountains thousands of metres high were pushed up. What was to become the wet tropics region was born. It was so long ago that only primitive plants, many of which have long since become extinct, grew on land. Their growth, however, was quite

Water-sculpted granite on the South Johnstone River

The roots of a penda tree grip granite boulders.

« Water-worn rocks of the Hodgkinson Formation on a beach in Daintree National Park luxuriant. As yet there were no conifers or flowering plants.

The great forces within the earth generated enormous heat. The pressure and heat changed the sedimentary rocks into metamorphic rocks. These are denser and the layering of the sediments is no longer discernible. For some 50 million years after these upheavals the region remained stable. The very high mountains were slowly eroded.

About 310 million years ago and continuing for the next 80 million years, there were periods when great heat was generated deep below the Earth's surface — as much as 30 to 50 km down. The heat was so fierce that it melted some of the rocks, creating pools of liquid minerals known as *magma*. Being molten, these gigantic pools were less dense than the surrounding solid rock and so began to rise, like air bubbles in water, only infinitely slowly. As these pools, called *batholiths*, came close to the surface they cooled little by little. The result was that they became ever more viscous and, eventually, again very slowly, solidified into rock — granite rock. None of the batholiths reached the surface at that time, although some rose to within 2000 m of it. Because these granites cooled so slowly they are composed of large crystals and therefore have a coarse-grained appearance.

Beginning about 230 million years ago, and for the next 100 million years, the region was again stable and a place of tall mountains. Erosion inevitably continued and several thousand metres of rock were worn away. The softer rocks of the Hodgkinson Formation eroded more quickly than the hard granite batholiths embedded within them. As the Hodgkinson rocks were stripped away, the batholiths were exposed and became mountains themselves. They remain to this day. Mounts Bartle Frere and Bellenden Ker are the highest, but other granite mountains occur the full length of the wet tropics — from Paluma to Black Mountain, both of which are also granite. Rocks of the Hodgkinson Formation can easily be seen at Barron Gorge and other places near the coast.

Towards the end of this era of stability, about 150-120 million years ago, great changes occurred in the planet's plant and animal life. The first flowering plants appeared. These are the "modern" plants — the ones that make up most of the plant populations in the temperate and tropical forests, the savannahs, the grasslands and the spinifex plains. These are also the plants that provide us with most of our foods and medicines. Mammals and birds, the "modern" animals, also first appeared in this era. It was the formative period for the wet tropics as we know it today.

Buckled and folded rocks of the Hodgkinson Formation

Close-up of partially eroded granite

A granite stream bed

The next major geological upheaval occurred between 100 and 65 million years ago. It was an event that affected the entire east coast of Australia.

During that time the eastern edge of the continent warped upwards, forming an almost continuous series of mountain ranges and tablelands. This watershed was just a few kilometres from the coast in some places but in others was several hundred kilometres inland. High plateaus were thrown up between mountain ranges (which today survive as the Great Dividing Range) and the sea. Erosion by the eastward flowing streams transported sediments from the tablelands and mountains, onto the coastal plain, which gradually grew wider. The eastern edge of the system of ranges and tablelands is called the Great Escarpment. In some places Escarpment and Divide almost meet, as they do near Cairns. In other places, such as in central-eastern Queensland, they are hundreds of kilometres apart. The classic east-west sequence of alluvial coastal plain, Great Escarpment, tableland and Great Divide is most clearly seen between Innisfail and Cairns — from the coastal plain, up the Escarpment along the Palmerston, Gillies or Kuranda Highways to the Atherton Tableland. On the Tableland's western edge is the Herberton Range — part of the Great Divide. While the Atherton Tableland is the best known, there are other rainforest-covered tablelands to the north and south of it. The formation of the Great Escarpment and the Great Divide close to the sea and the virtually constant moisture-laden trade winds created the conditions that allowed tropical rainforests to flourish here.

The top of Windin Falls

The last great event that literally shook the wet tropics occurred very recently — between 3.5 million and 15 thousand years ago. It happened mostly on the Atherton Tableland and involved scores of volcanoes. The oldest, and the ones that caused the greatest changes, were shield volcanoes. When they erupted, the lava flows were so copious and wide that they filled river valleys and ravines and generally covered the existing landscape. These volcanoes can still be seen as gently sloping hills near the townships of Atherton, Tolga and Malanda. The lava flows solidified into basalt rock, which in turn weathered into the deep, red-brown fertile soils that characterise the Tableland. In other places, the basalt is visible as columns of dark rock, especially where they are exposed by the wear of rivers such as in the North Johnstone and Tully River Gorges.

Scoria rock

More capricious in their eruptions, and with only local effect, were the cinder cones. A cinder cone is formed when volcanic gases explode from underground creating a vent. The explosions hurl huge quantities of lava and gas high into the air. The lava solidifies in the air and becomes riddled with holes and passages from the bubbles of gas it contained. The resulting rock, called *scoria,* looks somewhat like Swiss

A creek tumbles over a wall of columnar basalt to the Tully River.

« Windin Falls cascades over a granite precipice.

The Tully River runs in a bed of basalt rocks.

A rock pool on the Tully River

The Tully River

Close-up of basalt

The North Johnstone River winds through basalt hills.

cheese and is light in weight. A great deal of the scoria falls back to earth close to the vent where it builds up as a cone of cinders. There are numerous cinder cones, which are not very high, on the Tableland. The Seven Sisters (which is actually ten cones), Mount Quincan near Yungaburra, and Mount Wongabel near Atherton are all cinder cones. Because this volcanic activity was very recent, some estimates say as little as 15 000 years ago, the scoria has not yet extensively weathered into soil. Yet ground covered with the bouldery, pebbly rock does support rainforest, as can be seen at the Curtain Fig near Yungaburra.

The origin of other spectacular formations was even more violent. When molten lava welling up from below meets ground water percolating down, great volumes of superheated steam are created. The pressure that builds up is so great that eventually it is released in a massive explosion. A crater as much as 2 km across and maybe 100 m deep can be ripped out of the earth. Volcanic rock ejected by the explosion falls back to the ground, forming an elevated rim around the crater. It is just a one-off explosion and not a continuing eruption. In time, the crater fills with water and becomes a lake. The surrounding rocks weather and the resulting soil supports luxuriant rainforest right to the water's edge. Lakes Barrine, Eacham and Euramoo, formed about 95 000 years ago, are such crater lakes, known as *maars*. Lake Barrine is the largest — 1.5 km across at its widest and 65 m deep.

An equally violent explosion, but one involving only gas, can blast a deep vent out of the rocks. All that remains after the explosion is a deep cylindrical hole, which often fills with water and is called a *diatreme*. Only one occurs in the wet tropics, at Mt Hypipamee — its sheer walls drop 55 m to the water which is a further 87 m deep.

The volcanic activity, which may resume at any time, is the most recent event in a geological history that had its origins 420 million years ago, when the first silt from an ancient continent began to fill the deep Hodgkinson Basin.

A diatreme (a volcanic crater) at Mount Hypipamee

Lake Eacham, a crater lake in the rainforest

ORIGINS OF THE RAINFORESTS

Scaly Tree Ferns

Of all the stimulating aspects of the wet tropics rainforests, the story of their origins is the most exhilarating. It involves the gathering of evidence, from not only north-east Queensland, but many other regions of Australia, some of which are now deserts. Parts of the puzzle lie on other continents. The story reaches back about 120 million years, to a time when all the world's continents were joined together; when the present rainforests' principal plants, the flowering plants, first appeared. To piece the story together, scientists must search clays, coal, peat and other deposits for fossils. Much of the story was revealed by the study of microscopic fossilised grains of pollen, and was then fleshed out by examining beds of fossil flowers, leaves, stems and fruit. It is a botanical detective story without parallel.

Hope's Cycad

« Tree ferns on the edge of the rainforest

JURASSIC

Long before the first appearance of the flowering plants (between 200 and 144 million years ago), in a period geologists call the Jurassic, today's wet tropics, and much of the rest of Australia, were covered in rainforest. But it was a very different kind to the one that grows there today. There were, as yet, no flowering plants. The trees reached gigantic proportions but all of them were slow-growing conifers — pine trees. They belonged to a group called southern pines, that is, those that thrived in the southern hemisphere. They are quite different from the classic northern hemisphere pines, which have needle-like foliage and woody "pine" cones.

Fruit of a Brown Pine

The southern pines were mostly Araucarias and Podocarps, whose living descendants still grow in many parts of Australia — the kauris, hoop pines, brown pines and their allies. These trees rose out of an understorey of palm-like cycads and a great variety of ferns — the huge, spreading tree ferns among them. This luxuriant vegetation thrived for many millions of years in a moist, benevolent climate. There was a great abundance of food for the animal life, which was dominated on land by the dinosaurs. In north-eastern Australia, during this time, the rocks of the Hodgkinson Formation were eroding, exposing the underlying mountains of granite.

Leaves of a Kauri Pine

Giant Bull Kauris. During the Jurassic Period, Australian rainforests were dominated by tree ferns, cycads, kauris and brown pines. These species still grow in the wet tropics.

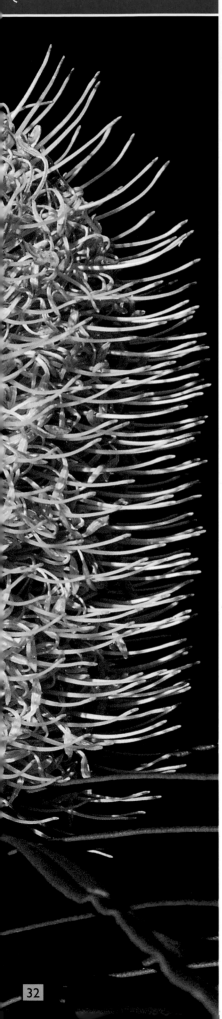

CRETACEOUS

The period that followed the Jurassic is called the Cretaceous. It began 144 million years ago and lasted for more than 78 million years. Although the Jurassic was a stable period, one of stagnation even, the Cretaceous saw great upheavals and change. At the beginning of this period, dinosaurs reached their greatest diversity, the peak of their evolutionary development, as did the southern pines, ferns and cycads. The continents, although still connected, began to rift, breaking up into their different masses. Those of the southern hemisphere — South America, Africa, Australia and Antarctica as well as smaller fragments — are collectively called Gondwana after an ancient kingdom in central India. Those in the northern hemisphere have been named Laurasia, which is a contraction of St Lawrence Basin (in North America), Europe and Asia. In the mid-Cretaceous, the dinosaurs and other reptiles began to decline. The dinosaurs were extinct by the end of the Cretaceous, about 65 million years ago.

As the reptiles began to decline, other animal groups, such as mammals and birds, arose. About 120 million years ago saw the emergence of the first true flowering plants. The advance of the flowering plants over the pines, cycads and others lay in their reproductive system, their flowers, and also in their leaf structure. The details of this are too complex to deal with in this account. In their eventual, full unfolding, the flowering plants diversified into giant trees as well as ephemeral herbs, grasses as well as orchids, and palms as well as lilies. In fact, they embrace all the brilliantly-coloured flowers, and most of the plant foods we eat. Today there are some 235 000 species of flowering plants, but only about 700 of conifers and cycads combined.

The first of the flowering plants, however, appeared when the pines and others still clothed the land. Then the events that led to the eventual extinction of the dinosaurs created niches for the rapid spread of the more vigorous flowering plants and with them the mammals and birds. The modern plants and animals began their conquest of the planet.

The flowering plants arose in the southern hemisphere, in western Gondwana, an area that is now west Africa and eastern South America, which were still joined together 120 million years ago. In 5 to 10 million years the flowering plants, had diversified to such an extent that they dominated the land. The equable climate of the time encouraged the formation of rainforests. A hundred million years ago, when the continents were drifting apart, much of Australia was covered by rainforests of flowering plants, including its northeastern corner, where rainforest has grown to a greater or lesser extent ever since. Unlike the dinosaurs, the Jurassic vegetation of southern pines, cycads and ferns did not become extinct. They continued to maintain a foothold in Australia, many in the rainforests. The kauris growing in the wet tropics today are not noticeably different from those that grew on the continent 175 million years ago.

TERTIARY

When the period after the Cretaceous, called the Tertiary, began 66 million years ago, Gondwanan rainforests were well established over most of Australia. The continents were separating widely, and, by about 45 million years ago, Australia was an island. The flowering plants, from then on, evolved in isolation until about 15 million years ago, when Australia, in its drift northwards, came into contact with the island chains of southern Asia.

For the late Cretaceous and early Tertiary, the fossil record is patchy. This changed dramatically during the Eocene Epoch, a subdivision of the Tertiary Period, which stretched from 58 to 36 million years ago. Most Australian fossils are dated to the period between 50 and 45 million years ago. Fossil pollen and beautifully preserved leaves, flowers and even fruits have been found. They have been discovered in many parts of the continent, but mostly in the south — a long way from the present day tropical rainforests in both distance and climate. Some important finds are in what is now desert, south of Lake Eyre in South Australia.

From the study of these fossils, it has been established that during the Eocene most of Australia was covered in tropical rainforest. One of the most intensively studied fossil deposits is near Anglesea, not far from Melbourne in southern Victoria. Discoveries there reveal that the rainforests of 45 million years ago may have been as diverse in plant species as those of today, perhaps even more so as many species of that epoch are now extinct. These ancient forests also contained many kinds of trees that are closely related to ones still growing in north-east Queensland, including the walnuts, bollywoods, silky oaks, ebonies, possum wood, flame trees, quandongs and a rainforest casuarina, as well as southern pines and cycads. Some fossil leaves and fruits of the silky oaks of 45 million years ago have the same characteristics as those found in north-east Queensland today. The rainforest growing at Noah Creek in the Daintree region today is very similar to the one that grew at Anglesea, 45 million years ago.

« Flowers of the White Banksia. The ancestors of the banksias grow in the wet tropics rainforests.

FOUR SPECIAL FAMILIES

Among the families of rainforest trees, both fossil and living, four are especially noteworthy, as they give Australia's tropical rainforests much of their particular character. Two of these families, while originating in the rainforests, broke out of this environment and adapted to the dry conditions that eventually overtook the continent. These families gave rise to the eucalypts, bottle brushes, banksias, paperbarks, grevilleas and their kin — the trees and shrubs that characterise most of the Australian forests that exist today,

Lomatia Silky Oak flowers

A large ant on Hill Banksia flowers

White Banksia

Flowers of the Ivory Curl Tree — a rainforest silky oak

Flowers of a Spice Bush — a kind of silky oak

Flowers of the Wheel-of-fire — a species of Silky Oak

woodlands and heaths. Their ancestors still live in the north Queensland rainforest.

Of these four families, the Proteaceae, which in rainforest are mostly trees called silky oaks, are the most Australian in their distribution, though not exclusively so. It is not inconceivable that this family first appeared in Australia, in rainforest, about 70 to 80 million years ago, and from there spread to the other southern hemisphere continents. Only a very few species migrated to the northern hemisphere. Of the world's 1700 living species of Proteaceae, 1100 grow in Australia. Of the non-Australian species, the Proteas of South Africa are the best known.

About 50 species of silky oak grow in the north Queensland rainforests. Some of these, such as the Fish-tail Silky Oak, and the Lomatia Silky Oak are close to, even indistinguishable from, the ancient trees of the Eocene Epoch. The silky oaks are not well-known trees, restricted as they are to the wilds of north-east Queensland. The well-known Australian Proteaceae are the banksias, grevilleas, hakeas and their dry-country allies. The link between the ancient silky oaks and the more modern banksias and grevilleas has been well established — the silky oaks are the direct ancestors of the modern forms.

Close-up of the flowers of a Northern Silky Oak

« Leaves of the Fish-tail Silky Oak of today's rainforests are indistinguishable from fossil leaves 40 million years old

An undescribed species of rainforest tree of the myrtle family, commonly known as Stockwellia

This Stockwellia and some other rainforest myrtles are probably the ancestors of the eucalypts, paperbarks, bottle brushes and their allies.

The myrtle family, the Myrtaceae, follows a similar pattern. It also arose in Gondwana, though perhaps not in Australia, but it spread a lot further afield than the silky oaks. This family also contains important and distinctive rainforest trees, both in the fossil record and in today's rainforests. The lilly pillies, satinashes, and pendas are all myrtles. One undescribed species of myrtle, a gigantic tree growing in the Bartle Frere–Bellenden Kerr region, is of special interest. It shows many of the characters in its leaves, flowers and fruits that are considered ancestral to another great group of modern Australian plants, the eucalypts — the gum trees. Other modern myrtles are tea trees, bottle brushes and paper barks. Their ancestors are also in these rainforests.

The first banksias and eucalypts were found as fossils dated to 36 to 40 million years ago. There were few species with restricted distributions. They had adapted, not to dry conditions, for Australia was still clothed in rainforest, but to poor soils: scoured, leached soils low in phosphorous and other plant nutrients. The plants' adaptations were tough leathery leaves and woody seed capsules which are so characteristic of the eucalypts and banksias of today. For many millions of years, these few species remained in the rainforest. When the Australian continent began to dry out, about 20 million years ago, it so happened that those plants adapted to infertile soils could also withstand long dry periods. Their tough leaves minimised water loss. The soft-leaved rainforest plants could not adapt and disappeared from the more arid places. In the absence of the lush species, those with leathery leaves, especially members of the silky oak and myrtle families, proliferated and diversified into thousands of species all over the continent.

Flowers of the Black Bean tree

Gymnostoma australianum is ancestral to the casuarinas.

« Stockwellia tree

Another great Australian group of plants of the modern epoch, one also adapted to dry conditions and with the greatest diversity of all, is descended from rainforest trees as well. These are the wattles. Their ancestors have not yet been established. Undoubtedly they are leguminous plants from the rainforest, such as the Black Bean, perhaps.

But the casuarinas, the river oaks and desert oaks, also characteristic of dry areas, have a clear ancestor still living in north Queensland's rainforest. It is also a so-called "oak" with the scientific name of *Gymnostoma australianum*. It has been found as a fossil in Anglesea and still grows at Noah Creek and other parts of the Daintree rainforests. Its foliage is a brighter green and its candelabra-like branching is simpler in pattern, but otherwise it is clearly recognisable as a casuarina, a river "oak".

The ancestors of the plants that give the very texture, the feel, the smell and even our emotional attachment to Australia, still thrive in the moist forests of this small corner of the continent.

One large and important family of rainforest trees, on the other hand, never left the rainforest. These are the laurels, which include the great variety of walnuts, bollywoods and others. Their fossil history has been difficult to trace, for their pollen has not been preserved. Fossil leaves, however, show that they were as important a part of the rainforest of 45 million years ago as they are now. But none adapted to either poor soils or a dry climate.

The flower of *Austrobaileya scandens*, one of the most primitive flowers known, is pollinated by a species of fly.

Fallen fruit of *Austrobaileya scandens*

The Idiot Fruit belongs to a primitive species of tree.

PRIMITIVE PLANTS

The ancestral plants, such as the Fish-tail Silky Oak and *Gymnostoma* are clearly ancient, their great age confirmed by the fossil record. Other plants in the wet tropics are primitive, some even more so than the ancestral plants, but not necessarily ancient, since their fossils have not been found. Primitive flowering plants have very simple structures. The flowers are of the most basic type and leaf veination has no clear pattern.

Flower of the China Pine

As well as having a rich variety of ancestral plants, Australia's living tropical rainforest has more primitive species than any other. A vine called *Austrobaileya scandens* is of particular interest. Its pollen closely resembles a fossil pollen considered to be the earliest known from a flowering plant — one that lived 110 million years ago, only a few million years after flowering plants first appeared. From this it can be inferred that *Austrobaileya's* flowers are very similar to the first on earth. The retreat of the rainforest, in the face of increasing aridity that began 20 million years ago, was a very, very slow process. The continent did not reach its present condition until about one million years ago. Even five million years ago, most of eastern and south-eastern Australia was still rainforest.

All this time Australia had been an island drifting north. It was not until 15 million years ago that the continent rammed into the southern Asian island chain that is now Indonesia. Sea levels since then have fluctuated, and at times the continents were virtually joined by a land bridge, enabling the interchange of plant and animal species between them.

Asia already had rainforests that had Gondwana elements. India, originally a fragment of the southern hemisphere Gondwana, had detached and drifted north, eventually becoming part of Asia. It arrived with Gondwana rainforest which spread rapidly through southern Asia, mixing with northern hemisphere species.

Flowers of the Bolwarra, a primitive plant

AUSTRALIAN ORIGINS

Native banana (right) and native ginger are thought to have invaded Australia from Asia.

Until the 1960s and 1970s, it was thought that all of Australia's tropical rainforest had flowed onto the continent from Asia, after the time of first contact. But, as the fossil record has shown, the Australian rainforests were firmly established well before this event. An Asian influx first seemed likely because far more species in plant groups common to both continents were found in Asia than in Australia. For example, the wild peppers are a group of about 2000 rainforest vines, only 12 of which occur in Australia's wet tropics.

It has now been established that this does not necessarily mean that the plants migrated from north to south. They migrated in both directions. A case in point is the ebonies. There are some 85 species in Malaysia's forests, and 500 in the world. Of these there are only seven in Australia's northeast. But then many species of ebony were discovered in fossil deposits in southern Australia, demonstrating that there was a rich flora of them long before the two continents became connected. Similarly, species of climbing palms — called wait-a-while or lawyer canes in Australia, and rattans in Asia —

Tick Orchid

thrived in Australia's rainforests many millions of years before the collision with Asia. It could well be that those and other species migrated from Australia into Asia where they radiated rapidly into many species.

Other evidence that Australia's rainforests resisted invasion from the north is the fact that one of the dominant families of the Asian rainforest, a group of hardwoods called Dipterocarpacaea, never managed to penetrate into Australia. They came only as far south as New Guinea.

Nonetheless, some species undoubtedly infiltrated the Australian rainforests, and enriched their diversity. Wild bananas and gingers, rhododendrons and some others are thought to have reached Australia after the time of contact. Perhaps even the most highly evolved of all plants, the orchids, entered Australia then. Of the world's 30 000 or so species, only 660 occur in Australia.

Considering all the evidence, therefore, it can be said that Australia's tropical rainforests are truly Australian in character. They are not a recent addition from the north.

« A scrambling fern

King Fern, the largest fern in the world

Lichen on a tree trunk

Lichen

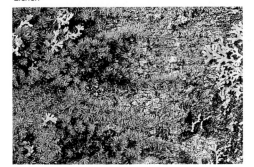

Moss and lichen

Australia's present-day tropical rainforests are remnants, fragments of the great Gondwana forests of 45 million years ago. They contain many primitive and ancient species. Words such as fragments and primitive suggest some token relic, a stagnating shadow of the once great forests. In terms of the area once covered by rainforests, the wet tropics rainforests are certainly fragments. But the forests themselves are not stagnating, they are dynamic in their diversity, and vigorous in their complexity. All that is needed is a moist, warm climate, and for humans to step aside, and nothing would stop them from conquering tropical Australia again.

Primarily a kingdom of flowering plants, Australia's tropical rainforest also embraces a host of other plant types. From the first land plants — the liverworts, mosses and lichens — to the ferns, cycads and southern pines, and from the most primitive lycopods to the most evolutionarily advanced orchids, they all find a place here. Poised on the rainforest borders are its descendants, the eucalypts, paperbark trees, banksias and grevilleas.

When you walk about in these forests, or look over them from a vantage point, you sense the power and mystery of these places, where every niche is filled to overflowing with plants competing for light and nutrients. How much more absorbing and exciting they seem when you realise that they are the direct descendants of ancient Gondwana forests, when you know about the earth's upheavals that formed the land, and the volcanic action that enriched the soil, and how they support a spectacular array of animals. Here the planet's heartbeat can be felt as in few other places.

Lycopodium cernuum

Flat Fork Fern, one of the first plants to colonise the land

Raindrops on moss with spore capsules

BIOLOGICAL DIVERSITY

In one hectare of rainforest, like this type in Wooroonooran NP, there are more species of tree than in the whole of North America.

It has long been known that the tropical rainforest is the most structurally complex habitat, inhabited by the greatest number of species of plants and animals that has ever existed. One scientist, in an effort to express this majestic and bewildering phenomenon, had to resort to unscientific language. He called rainforest the "apex of creation".

Early European explorers and scientists, accustomed as they were to the comparatively simple temperate forests, were intimidated by the luxuriance and vitality of the tropical forests, which were unlike anything they had known before. The German explorer and scientist Alexander von Humboldt, who travelled through South American rainforests between 1800 and 1804, was so overcome by the diversity of species that he wrote: "The excessive diversity of the flora and its richness in flowering plants forbid one to ask 'what is the composition of these forests?'"

Charles Darwin, contemplating the variety of beetles in a Brazilian rainforest in 1832, wrote in Voyage of the Beagle: "It is sufficient to disturb the composure of an entomologist's mind…".

Science and scientists eventually came to terms with the complexity and diversity of tropical rainforest and even became excited by them. But it took time. The forests' canopy is one of the last great natural frontiers to be explored. Its serious exploration and study did not begin until the early 1980s, and even now is in its infancy. The stimulating writings of today's scientists contrast greatly with the almost fearful accounts of many of the early explorers.

Jewel beetle

« Bark of a Khaki Bark Walnut

Len Webb, the father of rainforest ecology in Australia, calls tropical rainforests "the quintessence of life's mystery and power". He also wrote:

"They appear turbulent and sombre, yeasty and enduring, immense, indifferent, chaotic and mysterious. Yet not so mysterious that they inhibit rational thoughts about them. They are wild for exploring and thinking, because they have a quality of richness and timelessness that puts us in touch with genesis and for which we have no vocabulary... If we do not hear or see their silent machinery of species-making, we sense its potency."

The British botanist, E.J.H. Corner, wrote in the 1960s:

"I measured my significance against the quiet majesty of the trees. All botanists should be humble. From tramping weeds and cutting lawns they should go where they are lost in the immense structure of the forest. It is built in surpassing beauty without any of the necessities of human endeavour; no muscle or machine, no sense organ or instrument, no thought or blue-print has hoisted it up. It has grown by plant-nature to a stature and complexity exceeding any presentiment that can be gathered from books."

Rainforest is the most diverse habitat on land. (photo: Belinda Wright)

Giant Bull Ant

When you enter a tropical rainforest, you do not need facts and figures to tell you that you are in a habitat with more species than any other. You can feel it in the very vibrancy of life. You can see it all around, in the variety of trees, vines and ferns, in the butterflies fluttering around a flowering tree, in the frogs along a stream and so many other ways. Nonetheless, the statistics are not merely impressive — they are truly mind-bending.

In the 1970s, it was estimated that some two million species of plants and animals lived on the planet. The figure was arrived at by counting all the known species, then adding the number that various experts thought were still to be found. At least half of the species were thought to live in tropical rainforest, even though they take up only a small fraction of the earth's surface.

This figure had to be drastically revised in the light of findings in the early 1980s, when scientists first started to look closely at the rainforest canopy. On the basis of these studies, it was calculated that as many as 30 million species of invertebrates alone could exist in tropical rainforests. Just one group of 19 trees in a Panamanian forest yielded 1200 species of beetles. Another study carried out in a South American forest found that a single canopy tree was host to 54 species of ants — more than found in the whole of Britain. The greatest diversity of

Ulysses Butterfly

trees found so far is in the Peruvian Amazon, where nearly 300 species grew on a single hectare. The whole of Europe north of the Alps has only 50 species of native trees, and eastern North America only 171 species. Of all existing 235 000 species of flowering plants, two-thirds are found in the tropics.

The total number of living species of plants and animals is still being debated by scientists, but even the most conservative estimate is now 10 million, with considerably more than half living in the world's tropical rainforests.

In Australia, where the species richness of the rainforest has not been studied as extensively, the figures are also impressive. Twice as many frog species live in the wet tropics than in the whole of the State of Victoria. There are more species of butterflies in these forests than in any other habitat. One-third of the country's marsupials, one-fifth of the birds, one-quarter of the reptiles, and two-thirds of the bats make their home in the wet tropics rainforests. Two-fifths of Australia's plants occur in this small area. The trees alone are so diverse that just one plot the size of a large suburban house and garden may contain 164 different kinds of tree. In contrast, a tall eucalypt forest of almost equal density is often dominated by just three or four species. More than 200 of Australia's approximately 250 species

« *Top to bottom:* Moth caterpillar; Green Leaf Beetle; Male Orchard Butterfly. There are more species of butterfly in rainforest than in any other habitat.

of ferns are found in the tropical rainforest of north-east Queensland.

These figures are difficult to arrive at. The identification of rainforest plants, for example, is a complex process mastered by few. Just enumerating the plant species of a given area, therefore, becomes a problem. When it comes to identifying insects the difficulties are even greater. Most species are small to microscopic and species numbers are even greater than for plants. The Queensland entomologist, Geoff Monteith, collected about 1500 species of beetles on a single collecting trip to Mount Bellenden Ker.

THE WORLD'S RAINFORESTS

Tropical rainforests circle the globe's tropics — Central and South America, west and central Africa, southern Asia, New Guinea and north-eastern Australia. Australia's tropical rainforests are only 0.3% of the world's total, but what they lack in area they more than make up for in significance. They are extensively studied by scientists from many parts of the world, and are protected by World Heritage listing. All tropical rainforests are shrinking daily and are in need of protection.

Australia's wet tropics have had rainforests of flowering plants growing within them for as long as these kinds of forests have existed. They contain the evolutionary history of the world's most complex habitat, from Gondwana origins to the present day, and hold many of the secrets of life itself.

Stinkhorn Fungus

Herbert River Ringtail Possum. One-third of Australia's marsupials live in the rainforest.

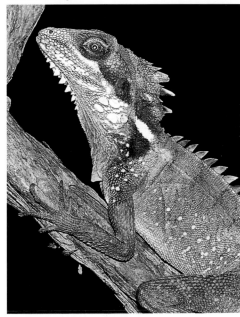

Boyd's Forest Dragon

Fungus growing on a rotting log

Primary rainforest, one that has gone through all successional stages to reach a self-perpetuating equilibrium, is rare in Australia. Most rainforests have been logged at one time or another or, if in the lowlands, devastated by cyclones. It takes hundreds of years to reach climax conditions. Parts of the Palmerston section of Wooroonooran National Park are climax forest: they are imposing places.

The sun has come out after a passing shower. The whole forest is fresh and sparkling. The trees, wet and dark, have towering, majestic trunks. Mosses and ferns clinging to rocks and trees shroud everything in a luminescent green. The largest trees, whose canopies reach well above the rest of the forest, rise straight and true for 40 m or more. Some have their trunks supported by elegantly-shaped plank buttresses. A fig tree of enormous girth has clusters of green fruit, flecked with dark red, sprouting from its smooth trunk. Fruits, some the size of a human fist, others no larger than a pea, lie scattered — scarlet, orange, yellow, blue, pink — over the sombre browns of the leaf litter. The winged seeds of a tulip oak, like miniature propellers, have whirled down to the ground. Among the gigantic trees grow others of a more modest size, but they, too, reach for the light with straight tall trunks. Thick coils of woody vines snake across the forest floor, then rise to the canopy where they smother the crowns of several trees. The ground cover is made up of seedling trees struggling to stay alive in the low light levels, the shade tolerant cycad *Bowenia spectabilis*, some ferns, and the occasional knotted tangle of vines that may have lost their grip on their supporting trees. It is not at all the impenetrable "green hell" of popular myth.

The voices of chowchillas, shrike-thrushes, whipbirds, riflebirds, Wompoo Pigeons and others reverberate through the forest with a clarity and resonance that would be the envy of any concert hall. At the canopy, there is a rush of wind, a commotion of leaves being tossed and branches bent, but on

PART TWO

HOW THE RAINFOREST WORKS

"Thus we have an actual struggle for life in the vegetable kingdom, not less fatal to the vanquished than the struggles among animals which we can so much more easily observe and understand."

ALFRED RUSSELL WALLACE
ABOUT RAINFOREST IN BORNEO IN 1855

the ground all remains still and serene. Only a few leaves and twigs, dislodged by the wind, drift downwards. A vine sways gently. Shifting shafts of sunlight illuminate orange fungi, a mossy log, an iridescent lizard or a palm frond.

Primary rainforest is a place of great vaulted spaciousness, of a grandeur above anything humanity could devise. It is one of the noblest assemblages of living, growing things on earth. It is also the most diverse habitat on land: only tropical coral reefs rival its complexity. And wherever you may see primary tropical rainforest, be it in north-east Queensland, southern Asia, west Africa or Central and South America, it will look very much like parts of Wooroonooran National Park. The species composition does vary from region to region, but the characteristics unique to rainforests are remarkably similar wherever these may be.

Most of us see rainforests along roads or close to human settlement, where the vegetation has been disturbed in one way or another. These regrowth, or secondary, rainforests are wild-looking places with impenetrable intertwining plants, and seem rampantly out of control. But even here are found recognisable structures and a discernible progression that in time will lead to primary forest.

Male Victoria's Riflebird

Fallen fruit of Blue Quandong

Red-throated Rainbow-skink

« A Grey Satinash in primary rainforest

WHAT THE RAINFOREST NEEDS

Tropical rainforests occur wherever conditions for plant growth are not just favourable, but optimum, with neither drought nor cold to eliminate sensitive species or limit growth. For *tropical* rainforest to flourish, rain must not only be copious but more or less evenly distributed throughout the year. The climate must also be warm.

Tropical rainforest needs at least 1500 mm of rain each year, without any rainless months. The monthly average temperature must be about 19°C or higher, without great daily fluctuations. Because of the rainforest's efficient nutrient turnover, known as the litter cycle, it is self-sustaining and can tolerate poor soils, as long as these are relatively well-drained. Permanently water-logged soils do not support rainforest. Another element that is necessary to maintain rainforests, by its absence rather than its presence, is fire. While Australia's extensive eucalypt forests are largely shaped by fire, rainforest is destroyed by it.

The crowns of rainforest trees do not intertwine. Each crown has its own separate space. (photo: Belinda Wright)

« Fallen fruit of a Brown Pine

TALL TREES

Mature tropical rainforest is dominated by trees with an average height of 30 to 40 m. An occasional giant, known as an emergent, projects another 15 m or so above the general canopy. Below the canopy are two or three more strata of trees, those that can tolerate the twilight, or younger trees waiting for an opening in the canopy so they can grow to maturity. There are forests growing within forests. Looking up from the ground, the crowns of the trees appear to interlock. But if you were to look down on them it would soon be apparent that each tree crown has its own space, separated from its neighbours by a narrow but clearly discernible gap. This phenomenon is called crown shyness. Even so, the canopy shuts out nearly all direct sunlight to the forest floor and so creates two separate realms. These two worlds are on average only 30 m apart, yet they are as different from each other as day is from night.

At treetop level there is brightness, fluctuation, and occasional violence. During periods of sunshine, the temperature may reach 33°C and usually drops to about 22°C at night. Humidity rises to about 90 per cent after dark, but drops to around 60 per cent during sunny days. The tree crowns are frequently buffeted by rain and gale-force winds.

CALM AND DARK

At ground level all is quiet and calm, and sometimes even gloomy. There is little or no wind. Humidity hovers around 90 per cent night and day, and the daily temperature fluctuates by only about 5°C. Rain which lashes the tree-tops reaches the ground in drips and trickles. Light intensity is only about one-hundredth of that at the canopy. So little light penetrates to ground level that only a few plants, those adapted to photosynthesise in perpetual gloom, can establish themselves. Other ground plants have solved this problem by becoming parasites, that is, by stealing the nutrients from other plants.

PHOTOSYNTHESIS

Vines, trees, ferns — all rainforest plants — compete for the light.

 All green plants need sunlight to grow. The colour of their leaves is given them by a substance called chlorophyll, and it is this chlorophyll interacting with radiant light from the sun that produces the energy for plant growth. This energy is used to produce plant food, mostly sugars, from carbon dioxide and water. Oxygen is a by-product of this chemical reaction and is released into the air, so supplying most of the oxygen in the atmosphere. This process, called photosynthesis, is the great engine that drives all life on this planet. It is what makes plants grow and ultimately all other beings are dependent on this force. So for rainforest plants to grow — and few other plants do so as fast or as luxuriantly — they must receive as much light on their leaves as possible. They must constantly compete for their place in the sun.

This competition is as fierce, as full of drama, as anything that goes on in the world of animals. We just cannot see it because it happens so very slowly. If we could see the life of plants greatly speeded up, if weeks became seconds for instance, we would see the plants pushing and shoving, clawing and strangling their way to an advantageous place. Evidence of these battles can be seen in tortured tree trunks, or severed limbs, overburdened with vines and epiphytes, that have crashed to the ground.

LEAVES

White Fig — one of the few deciduous trees in the rainforest

Flame Tree in flower

The leaves of rainforest trees range in size from 150 centimetres to just a few millimetres. But no matter what their size, the leaves of 80 per cent of species have one thing in common: they end in a distinctive point known as a drip tip. This construction helps to drain the leaves more quickly, which is of great advantage in the forests' frequent dampness, since dry leaves photosynthesise more efficiently than wet ones. Also, if the leaves were not drained, moulds, fungi, lichens and even mosses would grow on them more easily and inhibit photosynthesis even further.

Drip tip on ironwood leaf

In a few exceptional cases, green leaves are known to remain on a rainforest tree for ten years, but on average they live from 7 to 15 months and are shed irregularly. There are always exceptions. A few trees shed all their leaves at once, before a new flush of growth renews the cycle. The Curtain Fig, a form of the White Fig, sheds its leaves over a period of several weeks in spring. As the last leaves fall, new ones sprout, and the tree is bare for only a few weeks. One or two others, such as the flame tree, are without leaves for a month or more, when they are covered with brilliant red flowers.

The Bleeding Heart tree's leaves turn red before they are shed.

« A new leaf of the Hard Alder

Flame Tree flowers

LEAF COLOURS

In some species, the leaves ready to be shed become brightly coloured. The Bleeding Heart tree, for example, is so named because its heart-shaped leaves turn a pure red before falling. But since only a few leaves at a time become red, these trees do not stand out in the forest. However, many rainforest trees do have distinctive leaf colour changes, through another leaf characteristic unique to rainforests, although never on the scale of the great displays of autumn leaves found in the forests of some temperate regions.

The new, unfurling leaves of many rainforest trees, vines and shrubs are brilliantly coloured — pink, red, pale yellow, rusty brown, purple, golden. Only when fully mature do they turn green. Some species of satinash can be especially brilliant and make vivid patches of rose-red in the forest. New leaves on other species are densely hairy. It is believed that the pigments contain a fungicide and other poisons, and that the covering of hair protects the new shoots from fungal and insect attack when they are at their most vulnerable.

A flush of new leaves on a Plum Satinash

New leaves of a Red Carabeen

Moulds and fungi sometimes attack the soft part of a leaf; only the skeleton of the harder veins then remains.

New leaves of a Johnstone River Satinash

Blair's Malletwood

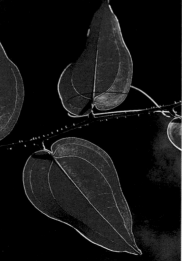

The vine, Austral Sarsaparilla

Davidson's Plum

BUTTRESSES

Tulip Kurrajong

Grey Carabeen

Grey Satinash

The diversity of species in tropical rainforest extends to all life-forms. Among the trees, for example, you rarely find two of the same species growing side by side. Yet, at first glance, this diversity is not at all apparent. The great majority have straight trunks without branches below the canopy. Their bark is smooth and thin and often covered with lichens and mosses. There are a few exceptions, like the rough, scaly bark of a Red Cedar and the pale, reddish-brown bark of a Paperbark Satinash. It takes a close look at the leaves, flowers and fruit, which are usually high in the canopy, to become aware of the variety of trees.

Perhaps the most spectacular of the rainforest characteristics are the gigantic plank buttresses that flange out from many of the tree trunks. These buttresses can be thin, delicate panels or huge slabs of wood 6 or 7 m long, roughly in the shape of a triangle. They are boards between the trunk and a horizontal root growing close to the surface. Some have a neat geometric form, while others are folded and twisted in fantastic configurations. A few species of trees, such as the Grey Satinash, which grows to an enormous size, have flying buttresses. These are like a series of arches that radiate out from and support the trunk. The base of the trunk itself may not even rest on the ground. When struck, plank buttresses often give a resonant sound which suggests their wood is stretched with some tension. These stresses or strains in fact help to support the tree on uneven ground and give it greater stability, especially in shallow soils. They need this extra stability, for trees with buttresses, and not all rainforest trees have them, are shallow rooted and lack a taproot.

Austrobuxus nitidus

Grey Satinash

« Unlike most rainforest trees, Shepherd's Ironwood has distinctive bark.

FLOWERING TRUNKS

Cauliflory is a flowering characteristic unique to tropical rainforest. Flowers sprout from the trunks of some trees, whereas in drier habitats flowers develop at branch tips. One of the most interesting cauliflorous trees is *Archidendron ramiflorum*. Large bunches of white, feathery flowers emerge from the length of its trunk, from ground level to a height of 7 or 8 m. Some of the flowers grow into even more striking fruits — bright red, elongated, coiled beans. When ripe, they split open revealing a bright yellow interior studded with shining, black seeds. The first Europeans to take note of cauliflory, in Java in 1752, could not believe their eyes. They thought the bunches of fruit sprouting directly from a solid tree trunk were parasites belonging to a different species.

Top left: Flowers of *Archidendron ramiflorum*
Top right: Flowers of Bumpy Satinash
Centre left: Flowers of *Pseuduvaria froggatti*
Bottom left: Fruit of *Archidendron ramiflorum*
Bottom right: Fruit of Bumpy Satinash

FLOWERS AND FRUITS

Brown Silky Oak

Wonga Vine

Johnson's Quandong

A few trees and vines in the rainforest have large colourful flowers that may cover their crowns in great profusion. At certain times of the year, when looking down on a forest from a vantage point, you can see the red of flowering Pink Silky Oaks, yellow of pendas, pale pink of corkwoods, white of October Glory Vines, and the orange and yellow of the Black Beans. There are colourful pinpricks

Climbing pandan

of flowering mistletoes, Umbrella Trees, Red Beeches, Powderpuff Lilly Pillies and others. Their nectar is harvested by butterflies, beetles and other insects, as well as sunbirds, honeyeaters, lorikeets and, at night, flying-foxes. The majority of rainforest trees, however, have small insignificant flowers which do not relieve the general greenness of the canopy.

Leichhardt Tree

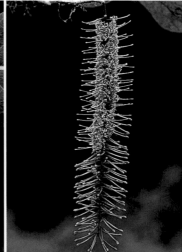

Sayer's Silky Oak

Powderpuff Lilly pilly

Bridled Honeyeater on the flower of a Pink Silky Oak

Umbrella Tree

« Top to bottom: Black Bean flowers; Jungle Vine; October Glory Vine

FRUITS AND SEEDS

The variety, colour and textures of rainforest fruits are unmatched by any other habitat. When walking through the forest, it is startling to see the trunk of a Bumpy Satinash studded with plum-sized white fruit, or a spice bush covered in bright orange fruit the size and shape of marbles, or a pittosporum bush glowing with orange and red fruit. Most fruits are high in the trees and become noticeable only when they fall to the ground. They may be a few orange fruit of an Austrobaileya Vine, or carpets of red Smith's Tamarind, Pink Jitta or Purple Satinash. Fruits are the jewels of the tropical rainforest.

A plant's fruit is the package that contains its essence, its seed. These packages, besides being conspicuous, often taste good and are attractive to many animals. Not all fruit, however, can be eaten by all animals. People, especially, are excluded from enjoying many of the rainforest's berries, "plums", "apples" and nuts. Since there is, as yet, little knowledge available as to which fruits are edible and which are poisonous, it is a good idea not to try any, no matter how tempting they may look. A forest ecologist, working specifically on fruit, was in the habit of tasting most he came across. He would take just the tiniest nibble, test it for flavour, then spit it out again. Not long after tasting the fruit of a spice bush, he collapsed with severe stomach cramps and intense nausea, and had to be hospitalised for a short while. Yet this same fruit is eaten by the forest rodents.

Many small flowers develop into large and colourful fruit such as the Brown Tuckeroo.

Pink Alder flowers are only a few millimetres across.

Brown Tuckeroo flowers are tiny.

SEEDS AND SEED DISPERSAL

Grey Carabeen

Fontain's Blushwood has very poisonous fruit.

To have its seeds fall immediately below it, and stay there, is of no benefit to a rainforest plant, especially a tree. The few seeds that would germinate would not grow into large trees in the dense undisturbed forest. The seeds need to be spread over as wide an area as possible, so that at least some can grow to maturity. Regeneration in rainforest is difficult enough, as seedlings can only grow where there is a break in the canopy after a tree fall. Seeds have to find their way to such places. Some, like the propellers of the tulip oak, or the silky parachutes of the sassafras and Milky Pine, drift on the wind. But most are transported by animals.

Yellow Beech

FRUITS AND ANIMALS

The chief dispersers of seeds are birds, with mammals playing a minor role. In Australia, reptiles and fish are not known to disperse seeds. About 40 bird species have rainforest fruit as a major part of their diet. They digest the outer covering then pass the seeds, which are often protected by a hard, indigestible coat. Birds can cover considerable distances between eating the fruit and voiding the seed.

This system of dispersal works perfectly for small-fruited plants. Their seeds find their way to openings in the forest and cleared spaces with the help of birds and, to a lesser extent, flying-foxes. The bats tend to spit out the seeds while feeding in the parent tree, and so are of no great help.

Harpullia rhyticarpa

Smith's Tamarind

Fruit of Hairy Red Pittosporum

« *Top to bottom:* Pink Jitta; Delarbrea; Fibrous Satinash

Top, left to right: Fruit of the cunjevoi; Topaz Tamarind; Scrub Breadfruit;
Centre, left to right: Native Lasiandra; Powderpuff Lilly Pilly; fruit of a lace-flower tree;
Boonjee Tulip Oak
Bottom, left to right: Small-leaved Tamarind; Red-bell Mischocarp; Spotted Catbird,
one of many fruit-eating birds, on its nest

A male Rose-crowned Pigeon.

But what of the large-fruited species, the big "plums", satinashes, walnuts, silky oaks and certain gardenias? These kinds of trees occur throughout tropical forests in considerable numbers and variety. For them, the cassowary is the main agent of dispersal. The size of a fruit that a cassowary can swallow is phenomenal.

This bird has no trouble with a good-sized apple, and few rainforest fruit are that large. Cassowaries are rare now and have disappeared from large areas of their former range. Will the large-fruited trees now also disappear from those places? Since they grow to be many hundreds of years old, it is difficult to be sure in the short term. Recent

studies have revealed that some mammals may help disperse large fruits. For instance, White-tailed Rats and Musky Rat-kangaroos will hoard large seeds. If these caches are forgotten, the abandoned seeds will germinate, if conditions are right.

Whether large or small, birds and fruit are closely tied together. Many seeds do not germinate readily unless they have passed through the digestive system of a bird. The bird's droppings, especially in the case of the cassowary, also provide fertiliser to speed the seedling's growth.

The fruits look good, many taste good, but as a food they do not rate very highly. They are low in protein, and high in carbohydrates and sometimes fat. Few birds and mammals eat nothing but fruit. Among mammals, flying-foxes come closest to an exclusively fruit diet, but even they will switch to nectar and pollen whenever the opportunity arises. Riflebirds and bowerbirds eat considerable quantities of insects, as well as fruit, as do honeyeaters and starlings. The cassowary eats fungi and any dead animals it can find. Only the fruit pigeons — the Wompoos, the Purple-crowneds, the Topknots and the Pied Imperials — are exclusive fruit-eaters. To get sufficient protein, these birds must eat enormous quantities.

Fruit is not a good food to bring young up on either. The smaller birds that include fruit in their diet raise their young on insects and spiders. Fruit pigeons, like all pigeons, produce a milk-like substance in their crops, and feed their young on that.

Cassowary with young

A Southern Cassowary eating Fuzzy Lemon-aspen fruit

« Top to bottom: A Fawn-footed Melomys eating an ivorywood fruit; a Giant White-tailed Rat has gnawed through these rock-hard Ebony Heart seeds; a Giant White-tailed Rat; a male King Parrot eating the seeds of a Black-fruited Walnut

While the fleshy outer covering of the fruit is a poor food, the seed is a different matter altogether. It is often very nutritious indeed. Many native rodents have discovered this and live on a varied diet of seeds. Among the birds, parrots and cockatoos will open the fruits, pierce the seed coats and eat the kernels. Sulphur-crested Cockatoos have such strong beaks that they can even bite through the thick, woody capsules of the northern silky oaks. For the plants this practice is disastrous. Parrots and rodents have in effect ignored the packaging, and penetrated the seeds' defences. Each seed-eater is a destroyer of potential plants. Luckily, seed-eating birds are few in number in the rainforest, and while feeding they spill, and therefore broadcast, a great many seeds.

FOOD PLANTS

Backscratcher Ginger

The tropical rainforests of the world are the source of many delicious fruits, nuts and spices, from bananas and rambutans, to pepper and nutmeg. Within Australia's rainforests grow many close allies of the prized

Fruit of the Atherton Oak

horticultural varieties. Bananas and a wide variety of gingers grow mostly in the lowland forests. Twelve different kinds of pepper vines ascend to the canopy. Nutmeg, with its red fleshy wrapping (the spice called mace), at times is a heavy crop on tall trees. Even fruits closely related to temperate-climate species, such as the true plums and raspberries, occur in the Queensland rainforest.

Unfortunately most of the native Australian species do not have the flavour of their cultivated counterparts. Our bananas

are small and gritty with seeds. The nutmeg and mace are insipid, as are the gingers. The peppers have only a faint, if pleasant, scent and flavour. The native plum of the true plum genus *Prunus*, is bitter and poisonous. Only the native raspberry, of the genus *Rubus*, is pleasant to eat.

However, other native rainforest fruits have the potential of being brought into cultivation. Lemon aspens are used as a tangy flavouring in bush tucker restaurants. The Davidson's "plum", which is not a true plum, and some of the tamarinds of the genus *Diploglottis*, while somewhat tart, can be made into jams, sauces and wines. Some nuts, such as the kernels of the Atherton Oak and the Ebony Heart, have a good flavour, but are difficult to extract from their rock-hard seed coats.

It must be stressed once again that unless you are *absolutely* sure of the identity of a fruit and its edibility, you should *not* try to eat it. There are many pitfalls. For example, several species of macadamia are found in the rainforest. At least one of them has large kernels that look very much like the commercial variety, but it is poisonous and people have died after eating them.

Top, left to right: One of the native peppers, *Piper rothianum*; Native Pleated Ginger fruit; Native Raspberry
Below: Boonjee Tamarind
Bottom, left to right: Davidson's Plums; Backscratcher Ginger

THE RACE TO THE SUNLIGHT

In the growth habits of the rainforest plants considered so far, none has impinged on another. But some species will overwhelm others or even kill them. Climbing plants, strangling trees and epiphytes all try to steal a march on their competitors in the race for the light.

Vines hoist themselves up to the roof of the forest very rapidly and in many different ways. They twine, hook, creep, grapple, scramble and thrust their way to the top. Of the many methods, five are the most common.

Twining vines

TWINER CLIMBERS

The simplest method is to twine around a tree trunk until the canopy is reached. Twiners grow quickly. One species was timed completing one revolution around its support in an hour and a half. Some of the largest, thickest vines in the rainforest are twiners, as is the primitive flowering plant Austrobaileya.

The tendrils of a watervine wind tightly around their support.

TENDRIL CLIMBERS

A more specialised but equally effective and rapid method of climbing is with tendrils. Tendrils are thin, pliable appendages grown only for climbing. They grow from the stems or from the tips of the leaves and reach out for something to fasten themselves to. Once they find a twig, a leaf or another support, a tendril winds quickly and tightly around it. A large climber will have hundreds, if not thousands, of tiny tendrils, each supporting the plant in an unrelenting grip. The so-called native grapes, or water vines, which grow to be among the largest vines, are tendril climbers.

Close-up of the hooks on a wait-a-while

HOOKED CLIMBERS

Another group of climbers use sharp hooks of various kinds. The climbing palms known as lawyer vines or rattans are a typical example. They have hooks and spines on their leaves and stems. As well, they grow thin, whiplike appendages studded with especially sharp, recurved hooks. The hooks and spines fasten themselves on any part of other plants and that way the palms claw their way to the canopy. Lawyer vines are common in the forest where they will hook into and restrain passers-by, who must stop and take time to disentangle themselves. In this way the palm became known as the "wait-a-while".

Pothos (top) and *Rhaphidophora* (above) vines climb by means of special clinging roots.

ROOT CLIMBERS

Some small vines such as pothos and certain ferns, as well as the giant pepper vines and climbing pandans, creep up tree trunks using specialised clinging roots. These roots grow laterally from the vines' stems and grip the tree bark, fastening themselves tightly to the tree by penetrating small fissures and cracks.

« *Top to bottom:* Lawyer canes or wait-a-whiles are palms that climb by means of hooks on long whip-like appendages; the growing tip of the Vicious Wait-a-while is protected by spines; the watervine climbs with long tendrils; stems of the Common Wait-a-while

SCRAMBLING CLIMBERS

The fifth group of climbers have no specialised appendages. They scramble to the top by the sheer vigour of their growth and by leaning and threading their long, supple stems on and through the branches of trees. The October Glory Vine, whose spreading canopy is covered with large bunches of white flowers in spring, is a scrambler.

A vine's route to the sunlight is a short-cut, for it does not have to spend many years building a solid, woody trunk as a support for its crown. But it can still be a long, convoluted journey. The stem of one Southeast Asian climbing palm, a kind of wait-a-while, was measured at over 200 m. The average length of a mature wait-a-while is, however, less than a third of that.

Ancient and large vines like this pepper vine may coil over the forest floor before ascending to the canopy.

Once a woody vine, known as a liane, has reached the canopy, it rapidly grows a large crown, rivalling that of the largest trees in size. In doing so, it often smothers and pushes aside the branches of the tree that supports it. Eventually the climber may become too great a burden for the host tree, and the entire vine and its supporting branches will then crash to the ground. Because of its flexible stems, the vine is rarely killed and will quickly grow up again, leaving a tangle of rope-like loops and knots as a legacy of its temporary setback. Old mature vines, which may have stems 25 cm or more in diameter, have no branches or support below canopy level. It looks as though they made their way up by some magic Indian rope trick, but what has really happened is that they have outlived their original support.

STRANGLER FIGS

Another group of plants has solved the problem of reaching the light quickly, even more ruthlessly. These trees, mostly species of fig, take a short-cut by germinating not on the ground but in a suitable place high up in another tree, where they receive enough light to grow vigorously. Strangler figs do not wait for an opening in the forest to begin the struggle upward for a permanent place in the sun. They start at the top and work their way down.

The fruits of strangler figs are great favourites with birds and flying-foxes, and these animals distribute the seeds throughout the forest. If a seed happens to lodge in a place where there are sufficient nutrients, in a tree fork perhaps, where dead leaves and other debris have accumulated, it germinates and quickly establishes a hold. The growing seedling sends roots 20 m or more down along its host's trunk. Before long, these aerial roots, looking like ropes and cables, reach the soil and grow rapidly. The seedling expands into a small, bushy tree standing in the canopy. Over the years the roots multiply, thicken, join together and tightly envelop their supporting trunk and the fig's crown overshadows that of its host. In the end, the host has its trunk completely engulfed, its leafy branches smothered, and its root system usurped. Gradually, remorselessly, the host is strangled and eventually dies, yielding its place to the more aggressive plant. Eventually, the original supporting tree's trunk rots away, leaving the strangler standing like a hollow tower, a tower that may grow to be among the very largest trees in the forest.

Top: Aerial roots of a Curtain Fig *Right:* The famous Curtain Fig at Yungaburra
Bottom, left to right: The strangling roots of a fig; a fig strangling a paperbark tree

There are several species of strangler fig. One is the Rusty Fig. The Banana Fig beloved by flying-foxes is another. But the grandest, most majestic of all the stranglers, and among the most impressive of all the trees, is the Curtain Fig, such as those found on the Atherton Tableland. As its name suggests, the aerial roots do not merely wrap around their host, but cascade down in sheets of intertwining stems, some thick and woody, others as fine as hair.

EPIPHYTES AND PARASITES

EPIPHYTES

The layer of small plants that is found at ground level in other habitats has had to migrate upwards to the light in rainforest: lichens, mosses, ferns and small flowering plants are forced to grow on the trunks and limbs of large trees. These plants, like the vines, are entirely dependent on the trees, but only for a foothold. They are not parasites, but epiphytes; that is, they take no nutrients from their hosts. Epiphytes festoon large trees, such as the emergents, in luxuriant hanging gardens that may contain more than fifty species of plants.

A large Basket Fern

Epiphytes usually attach themselves to their support with a network of clinging roots. This gives them a place in the light, but does not solve another problem: how to obtain the moisture and nutrients that other plants derive from the soil. A group of large ferns, known as staghorns, elkhorns and bird's nest ferns, overcomes that most effectively. They have two kinds of leaves, each with a different function. One kind is broad and rounded. Several together grow into a rosette around a tree branch or trunk. These rosettes grow in the shape of a basket that collects falling leaves and other organic material. This debris decays and so provides food for the growing fern and also soaks up and holds moisture. Some of these ferns grow baskets so large that they may collect half a tonne of humus complete with earthworms, millipedes and other organisms usually found in the soil. The ferns' other kind of leaves are narrow and a darker green. They carry out the photosynthesis and bear the reproductive parts, the spores.

Oak Orchid

The orchid Robiquetia tierneyana

Orchids, many of which are epiphytes, have solved the problem another way. They store water in fleshy leaves and swollen, even bulbous, stems. Their roots swell and absorb moisture from dew-laden air as well as from the rain. They somehow find enough nutrients in crevices in bark or in the dead leaves trapped among their tangled roots. More than 150 species of epiphytic orchids are found in Australia's tropical rainforest. These vary from tiny bark creepers to the gigantic clumps of King Orchids.

Plants that need to establish themselves high in the trees must have adaptations for their seeds and spores to be dispersed, so that they lodge in the right places. Seeds that are heavy and fall to the ground would be useless. The spores of mosses and ferns are microscopic, and so light that they are carried by the wind. Similarly, orchids produce huge numbers of tiny seeds that float on the air currents. A single orchid seed pod may contain as many as three million seeds. At least some are sure to land in places where they can germinate and grow.

Epiphytes can grow so profusely and so large that collectively they overburden their supporting tree branch, causing it to break and crash to the ground.

Elkhorn Fern

The Blue Orchid is a large epiphytic species.

« *Top to bottom:* Close-up of a Basket Fern; a Bird's Nest Fern with a Ribbon Fern growing from beneath it; an Elkhorn Fern

The "roots" of a Queensland Mistletoe penetrate their host's bark and tap into its sap flow.

PARASITES

A few other kinds of plants drop all pretence at being self-supporting. They have become parasites. One group, the mistletoes, establish themselves high up among the branches of trees. They still partially support themselves, in that they have green leaves, and therefore photosynthesise. But their roots drill into their host's bark, and so the plants help themselves to the moisture and nutrients that the tree gathers from the soil and then draws to its uppermost branches.

Another group of parasites lives at ground level. Because there is not enough light, they do not even photosynthesise, so they are pale and ghostlike, not green. They have no roots of their own, but use suckers to penetrate the roots of other plants, including many kinds of trees. Most common of these is the root parasite balanophora which pushes its flowers, borne on cones, through the leaf-litter in winter. The flowers are pale pink or yellow, while their leaves are mere scales, almost white. The whole structure looks more like a fungus, but a close examination shows a ring of male flowers, bearing white pollen, around a smooth, rounded knob which is composed of about a million female flowers. When the plant is not flowering, its tuber is completely obscured by the leaf-litter.

Mistletoe flowers

Competition among the plants for light is fierce, and gives the rainforest its very shape and structure. Below ground, the competition is just as ferocious. Trees, shrubs and vines enmesh the soil and leaf-litter with a fine network of roots vigorously searching for nutrients.

The next question is — how does the primary rainforest maintain itself? A large part of the answer lies in the rapid turnover of organic matter on the forest floor.

Flowers of the Queensland Mistletoe

The root parasite balanophora

Queensland Mistletoe

WHAT MAKES A RAINFOREST?

Tropical rainforest is a place where there are virtually no limits to plant growth; where trees are so dominant that forests grow within forests; where competition for their energy source, the light, is so intense that plants grow upon plants, that trees strangle each other and vines grapple and push their way to the canopy where they smother their supports. In a rainforest, trees may have buttresses, flowers may sprout from tree trunks and leaves unfold in brilliant colours. A rainforest is not a chaotic place but one where trees, vines, shrubs and epiphytes, together with all the animals they support, form a self-sustaining, dynamic association of species — the richest, most diverse on earth. It is also a highly efficient and stable community that makes greatest possible use of the energy from the sun and nutrients in the soil.

Above: Fallen fruit of the Buff Quandong
Left: Giant White-tailed Rat
Right: A large rainforest tree laden with epiphytes: lichens, mosses, ferns and orchids

RECYCLING

The leaves, twigs, branches and even whole tree trunks that constantly come down in the forest accumulate on the ground. Most of the time the debris is saturated with moisture, making it soft and spongy. This gives the forest a not unpleasant smell of decay — not the stench of large organisms rotting away, but a faint, musty scent; a whiff of the second of nature's energy-producing processes at work. The first, photo-synthesis, is driven by chlorophyll, the green stuff of plants, reacting with sunlight.

The second process is almost entirely carried out by fungi and animals. Many of them are minuscule, and the vast majority microscopic. Their work is performed in the layer of dead leaves and other organic matter lying on the ground, and in the top 10 cm or so of the soil. This breakdown of organic material into its component parts, which are then once again taken up by the plants as nutrients, is called the litter cycle. It takes place in just about all terrestrial ecosystems, but in the constantly moist and warm conditions of tropical rainforest, it goes on with speed and efficiency.

Skeleton leaf

LEAF LITTER

In tropical rainforests, 8 to 10 tonnes of litter falls on each hectare of land every year. It might seem that this amount of debris would produce mountainous heaps of leaves, branches and logs, but this is not the case. Under normal circumstances, only a thin layer of dead leaves covers the soil and only the most recently fallen branches and tree trunks lie on the ground. The exception is the immediate aftermath of a cyclone, when the ground may be strewn with an impenetrable mass of tangled vines and fallen trees. Even these accumulations, however, will rot away in 4 to 5 years. There are exceptions. The Grey Satinash, for example, may resist the attacks of borers, fungi and other organisms for decades.

In drier habitats, such as a eucalypt forest, the story is very different. Fallen trunks may lie in the undergrowth for a century or more, and if it were not for periodic fires the litter build-up would be enormous.

A Watkin's Fig has died and collapsed. It will be reduced to humus by the combined attacks of insects, fungi and micro-organisms.

« Litter accumulating on the rainforest floor is quickly broken down by vast armies of small and microscopic organisms.

An old buttressed tree has almost rotted away.

The larva of a wood-boring longicorn beetle

Centipedes invade the hollows and tunnels in dead wood.

The winged king cricket *Gryllotaurus bicornis*

In a sheltered patch of tall rainforest, the evidence of the litter cycle in action is all around. Old logs and branches are covered with fungi — outgrowths of orange barred with yellow; of black edged with red; of plain grey or brown. A large stump may be covered by a forest of delicate white fungi in the shape of umbrellas. The insides of fallen logs are tunnelled and excavated by insects, mostly beetles. When exposed, pill millipedes, opportunistic invaders of the insect tunnels, roll themselves into tight, shining black balls the size of marbles. Centipedes, predators on the insects and other invertebrates, also squeeze through the passages. Some of the tunnels will contain the pupae of large, spectacular species such as stag beetles and longicorn beetles, but most of the inhabitants are tiny. The larger tunnels are often the home of a lizard, a Spiny Skink, which lives only in and under damp logs, where it feeds on insects and other small animal life.

The giant wingless cockroach, *Panesthia sloani*

Passalid beetles and their larvae

A trapdoor spider of the genus *Homogona*

Termites, like these *Neotermes insularis*, are one of the few organisms that can digest wood.

The Spiny Skink lives in and around fallen logs.

FUNGI

The rotting wood is permeated by fine networks of white threads. These are the growing parts of the fungi, called mycelia, and are the major agents of decay. Mycelia spread rapidly through damp, softened wood and dead leaves. The mushroom or toadstool is only a small part of a fungus. This is the reproductive body that carries the spores, the equivalent of seeds in green plants. The growing mycelia can penetrate solid wood and consume it, but only slowly, a cell at a time. So, the greater the surface area of wood exposed, the more rapid the attack. Boring and tunnelling insects speed up the process, not only by opening up the wood, but also by carrying spores into their tunnels. Animals that hunt wood-boring insects accelerate decay even further. Many of the logs you will see on the ground have been pulled apart — reduced to chips by Striped Possums and White-tailed Rats, in their search for beetles and cockroaches. After a few months the chips will be reduced to humus. Long before this stage is reached, plant roots will have penetrated the rotting wood, extracting the nourishment as it is produced. One species of orchid, the Giant Climbing Orchid, specialises in living entirely off wood-decaying fungi. Between October and January, the 20 metre tall climbing stems produce masses of sweet-scented flowers.

Yellow-footed Antechinus

Fungi cover a rotting log.

THE FINAL BREAKDOWN

Not just fungi and woodborers are at work here. Peeling back a layer of dead leaves from the damp soil will expose a mass of minute jumping and wriggling animals. These are the larger springtails (insects), and amphipods (crustaceans). There may also be small cockroaches, beetles, ants, snails, slugs, and the end of an earthworm disappearing into the soil. Other organisms are so small that even a strong magnifying glass is of little help, but a microscope would reveal a world seething with small springtails, mites and nematodes. In north Queensland's rainforests very little is known as yet about these minute animals; most can only be assigned to broad categories. But the variety of species is enormous. In an English forest, which is much less diverse than tropical rainforest, 1000 animal species were found in a square metre of litter and soil.

Not only are there many species in the litter, most occur in numbers that defy the imagination. The weight of living animals in a forest may perhaps give a little insight into just how busy a place the litter zone is. In an Amazonian rainforest (no figures are available for Australia), all the living plants on a hectare of land weighed 1000 tonnes. All the animals, from jaguars and monkeys, birds and snakes, down to insects and soil organisms, came to 210 kg per hectare. Soil and litter animals accounted for 75 per cent of this weight. Since an average-sized bird weighs very many times more than a minute litter decomposer, imagine what great numbers and energy are constantly at work breaking down the fallen plant matter.

This cross-section through a rotten tree trunk shows how insects of various kinds have tunnelled through it. These damp recesses are then invaded by numerous fungi.

« Wood-destroying fungi

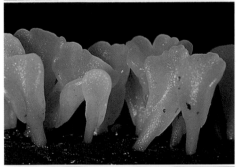

Various fungi which grow on logs and in leaf litter.

Just as the Striped Possum and the White-tailed Rat help in returning logs to the soil, so birds that constantly rake the ground like the chowchilla, Brush Turkey and the scrubfowl, help turn over the litter and hasten its breakdown. This is despite the fact that the birds eat a considerable number of the decomposers in the process.

The last stages of the breakdown of debris take place in the soil. The vital link here is not a microscopic animal, but the earthworm, a veritable giant in this world. The mass of partly-decayed particles of leaves and wood is consumed by the earthworms and then worked into the soil. So thorough are the worms, that nearly all the soil to the depth of 5 cm or more has passed through the alimentary tract of an earthworm at some stage. The final breakdown is effected by microbes, bacteria, fungi and algae. By this time the forest litter has been reduced to humus, a dark brown amorphous material without a trace of the structure and composition of its original components. All the nutrients that originally built the leaves and wood are returned to the soil.

This food is immediately taken up by the roots of the living plants. Even the largest trees have feeding roots close to the soil's surface, and often in the litter itself. Rainforests recycle themselves endlessly and efficiently, so efficiently that next to no minerals are leached out of the topsoil and litter, despite periods of prolonged and heavy rainfall. Streams sampled in mature rainforest contained little or no minerals derived from the soil. The litter cycle makes it possible for rainforest to grow to a climax community even on poor soil, in some places even on pure sand which itself does not contain enough nutrients to support such a forest.

Photosynthesis and the litter cycle, working in tandem, drive tropical rainforests to be the most efficient and prolific of land ecosystems. The litter cycle is largely instrumental in maintaining the equilibrium of primary rainforest. But what happens when this balance is upset — when a cyclone or landslide rips through a forest or, on a smaller scale, one of the great emergent trees is blown down in a gale?

A criss-crossing mesh of feeding roots of trees runs through the litter, absorbing the nutrients as they are produced.

The roots of a Pimply Ash (left) and a Hard Alder. Competition by the forest's trees for soil nutrients is fierce.

REGROWTH AND SUCCESSION

Even the greatest of trees, the largest of the emergents that may have lived for 800 or even 1000 years, must eventually topple. Its equilibrium, the balance between buttresses and a solid sturdy trunk on the one hand, and the weight of its crown and perhaps an overload of gigantic vines and tonnes of epiphytes on the other, will finally be upset. Also, the root system may be undermined by percolating water and slippage in the soil, particularly if the tree is growing on a slope.

THE FALL OF A GIANT

Imagine what happens when a centuries-old tree, of enormous girth and nearly 50 m tall, that has been growing on a hillslope of the Atherton Tableland, meets such a fate.

An unusually violent thunderstorm in early December has winds so strong that limbs are torn from trees and leaves stripped from their branches. The Red Carabeen's crown, which projects well above the forest canopy, is buffeted back and forth. Finally, with loud reports, its buttresses and roots snap and the tree crashes down. Its fall brings down a score of other large trees and smashes many smaller ones, as the tree rolls a little down the slope. Vines that had climbed up the emergent and then invaded some of the canopy trees are ripped down and take some of their hosts' crowns with them. The loud crashing sounds are drowned out by the noise of the wind, rain and thunder.

The morning after the storm is hot, still and sunny. There is a great devastation. The soil is exposed where the roots of the fallen tree, and those it knocked down, have been torn from the ground. The microclimate of the gap is suddenly very different from that of the same area when it was under the carabeen's umbrella. There is intense radiation from the sun where the light was once dim. The relative humidity drops from about 90 per cent to less than 60 per cent. The temperature of the top layer of soil rises from 20–25°C to 35°C.

Over the following weeks, which are mostly sunny with only occasional storm rain, many of the small trees in the seedling bank that grew on the forest floor are killed. Their leaves are burnt by the sudden hot, bright sunlight. Some of them have been struggling to survive in the gloom of the emergent's shadow for 30 or even 50 years, waiting for just such a gap to form. But for many it is too much, too suddenly. Those that can tolerate the direct sun, and those that are shaded by trees on the edge of the new clearing begin to grow quickly. All these seedlings and saplings are species that grow in the primary forest, of which the old carabeen was a part.

But another group of seedlings has sprung up and grows even more rapidly. None of their species lives within many kilometres of this new opening in the forest. They grow from seeds that had been lying dormant in the soil. Research has shown that this group of species, known as pioneers, has its seeds in the soil in all parts of the rainforest at all times. These seeds are small and hard and can withstand drying out. They may lie dormant in the soil for decades, perhaps even centuries. The exact time has not been tested, but it is known from other parts of the world that some seeds remain viable for thousands of years.

An ancient Red Carabeen in primary forest

« The tree with the pale stems is a celerywood, a pioneer species that grew up in a rainforest clearing.

SEED BANKS

In general, the primary forest species, known as climax species, have larger seeds that cannot lie dormant for any length of time. When they fall they must have the right conditions for germination or they will die. Because the seeds are larger, they have food reserves and when they do germinate, they

Seeds, in their pod, of a Black Bean tree, a climax species

have enough stored energy to send down a root system and put out the first few leaves. From then on, they grow slowly, and, when 1 or 2 m high, remain almost dormant as thin stems with just a tuft of leaves at the top. If no gap forms in 50 years or so they die, but are constantly replaced by newly germinating seedlings. So, when the old carabeen was felled by the storm and

created a gap of about 1600 sq m, there was a bank of seeds of pioneers in the soil and a bank of seedlings of climax species struggling to grow in the forest.

The two groups now race to consolidate their places in the opening and, in time, to fill it entirely. The heat and the increased light trigger the tiny seeds of the pioneer species to throw off their dormancy and germinate. Within a short time the new seedlings have caught up with those of climax species and within a year have overshadowed them.

Black Bean seedlings. The large seeds of climax species have enough stored energy to give the young trees a good start.

One of the first pioneers to appear on the exposed soil left by the old carabeen's demise is a small shrub with large, fresh-green, heart-shaped leaves covered with hairs that glint in the sun. Later, it will be adorned with equally attractive translucent pink-purple fruit. This is the Gympie Stinger which can inflict painful and, in extreme cases, even dangerous stings.

After a year or two the Gympie Stingers will be overtaken by the other pioneers: the Pink Ashes or sarsaparillas, several species of celery wood, Black Wattles, Brown Kurrajongs, Bleeding Hearts, mallotuses and a few others. Just one or two climax species, perhaps a Blue Quandong and a bollywood, will keep pace with the pioneers. In about ten years, when the carabeen has all but rotted away and has been reduced to humus that fertilises the new trees, these species will have formed a closed forest — a regrowth or secondary forest. The Gympie Stingers will have died. After another 30 or 40

Male Mueller's Stag Beetle on the flowers of a Pink Ash

years the other pioneers will also have completed their life-cycle and begun to die off. Their branches will wither, and their trunks will slowly rot away and collapse. This gradual removal of the canopy has a different effect from the sudden creation of a large gap when the old tree was blown over. The climax species receive more and more light, and over time replace all the pioneers. Several centuries will pass before another emergent grows in the carabeen's place.

The toppling of a centuries-old tree that creates a large gap in the canopy is rare these days, since nearly all of the forests have been logged, but pioneer trees just as readily invade artificial clearings. Most are seen along road edges and cleared areas where rainforest is allowed to regenerate. The pioneers must at first compete with virulent weeds — introduced grasses and legumes, and the vigorous, rambling, lantana. Originally from Mexico, lantana was introduced as a decorative garden

Fruit of the Brown Kurrajong showing the small durable seeds of a pioneer species

« Two kinds of pioneer trees in secondary forest: the straight-trunked White Basswood in the foreground and flowering Pink Ash in the background

plant by early settlers. However, given time — 40 to 50 years — the pioneers will win.

Apart from their different seeds, there are other striking differences between pioneer and climax species. Pioneers grow extremely quickly. The fastest growing of all trees is a pioneer tree from Malaysia called *Paraserianthsis falcataria* which can grow up to 10 m in a year. The wood of pioneers is usually pale in colour and light in weight. The balsa tree, whose very light wood is used in model-making, is a pioneer species from South America. Pioneer trees cannot tolerate shade and they are never found below the canopy of primary forest. Their crowns are open with a simple branching pattern. They produce seeds copiously from an early age. Leaves are short-lived and have few defences against insects and other foliage eaters. Pioneer species are few in number and do not live to a great age: fifty or sixty years perhaps.

Climax species, by contrast, grow slowly and their wood is often dense and dark in colour. They are shade tolerant and their seedlings and saplings are always found beneath the canopy. Their crowns are thick with intricate branching patterns. Seeds are larger, fewer in number and first appear only when the tree has reached its full height. Their leaves are long-lived, several generations often being found on the same tree, and can be tough or poisonous as a defence against the attacks of leaf-eaters. Climax trees have a great variety of species, many of which live for centuries.

A Topknot Pigeon feeding on the fruit of a celerywood, a pioneer species.

Pioneer trees, like the White Basswood and the pale-trunked Pink Ash in the background, have a simple branching pattern. They also have a short life span. The slower-growing climax species have established themselves beneath the pioneers and will eventually take over.

CHEMICAL WARFARE

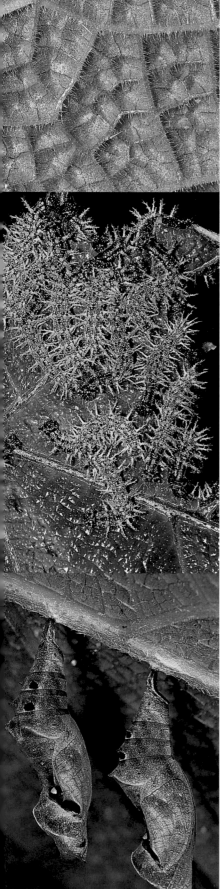

The rainforest's unlimited, constantly renewed, supply of fresh leaves seems at first a benevolent catering system for all leaf-eaters. Most are insects, but a significant number of mammals, such as the possums and tree kangaroos also eat leaves. The plants, however, are not that generous. In fact, a constant battle is waged between rainforest plants and the animals that eat them.

Fruit of the Poison Walnut.

TOXIC DEFENCE

To combat the unceasing onslaught on their leaves, most rainforest plants (in some places as many as 90 per cent of them), have developed toxic chemicals of one kind or another as a defence. These chemicals can be very potent and corrosive. The Poison Walnut, for example, has sap that is severely poisonous. When it comes into contact with human skin, it causes blisters, rashes, sores and swellings, as well as headaches and depression. The effect can last for as long as 12 days. The tree was avoided at all costs by timber-getters. The tarwood has a ready supply of toxic black sap. Some years ago a large specimen of this sturdy and handsome tree grew

along the esplanade in Cairns. People loved to park their cars in its shade, but sap dripping from nicks and cuts in the bark of its branches ruined the paintwork of many vehicles. The tree was eventually cut down.

The most extreme example of a plant's chemical defence is the Gympie Stinger. This tree is an unusual pioneer species, since most pioneers do not have toxic leaves. The translucent white hairs on the stinger's leaves, stems, and fruit are made of silicon — they are minute needles of glass. Each hair is tipped with poison and histamines. When you brush against a stinger, the crystalline hairs penetrate the skin, break off and stay there. The poison causes instant severe pain, which is reinforced by an allergic reaction created by the histamines. Because the hairs remain in the skin, the pain persists for weeks, even months. There is no known antidote. The sap of the cunjevoi, a succulent, large-leaved aroid that usually grows not far from a stinger, is sometimes recommended, but it does not help and is, in fact, a skin irritant itself.

Fruit of the Gympie Stinger

Fruit of the Tar Tree

« *Top to bottom:* Close-up of the stinging hairs of a Gympie Stinger; despite their toxicity, Gympie Stingers are eaten by several animals, like these caterpillars of the White Nymph; pupae of the White Nymph hanging from the leaf of a Gympie Stinger

Some plants exude a sticky, usually milky, latex which gums up the jaws of would-be leaf-eaters. Many species of fig have this sap in their leaves. Other leaves are simply unappetising because they are tough and leathery.

Male Cairns Birdwing

New tender leaves are soft and nutritious and therefore the most vulnerable, but these are given extra protection, both chemical and mechanical. The bright colours of new leaves contain extra poisons. The growing tip of the wait-a-while, the nutritious "cabbage" of this palm, is fenced in by long thorns. The velvet of the Velvet-leaf Bollywood is made up of a dense covering of fine hairs on the pale new leaves. The hairs are later shed. The growing tips of the tree fern, the "fiddles", also have a dense covering of hairs. Hairs and thorns are effective deterrents to most leaf-eaters. So to any leaf-eating animal, the tropical rainforest is far from being a tasty never-ending free meal. Instead, it is a perilous place full of poisons, sticky substances, spikes, and tough, hard-to-digest food.

SPECIALIST ANIMALS

Such is the forest's dynamic balance, however, that not even the strongest chemicals or toughest leaves make the plants totally immune from the jaws and digestive tracts of animals. As the plants developed

Gympie Stinger leaves can cause long-lasting pain. This small tree is a pioneer species.

their defences, insects and mammals evolved methods to cope with them. However, the plants have won a victory of a kind: the animals had to specialise as to which particular poison they overcame. Not all animals are immune to all plant poisons. For example, the caterpillars of many species of moth and butterfly feed only on a specific plant: the birdwing on the native Dutchman's Pipe Vine, the Ulysses on corkwood trees, the Red Lacewing on Lacewing Vines, and so on. The butterflies have turned the poison to their own advantage. When the caterpillars of the birdwing butterflies eat the leaves, they do not neutralise the toxins, but store them in their bodies. These toxins are retained when the caterpillar changes, first to a pupa, then to a butterfly which is now poisonous to predators. Birds, lizards and marsupial insect-eaters soon learn that the birdwing is poisonous, and leave the butterflies alone.

Not even the dreaded Gympie Stinger is safe from attack. The caterpillars of the White Nymph Butterfly eat the leaves of the several species of stingers exclusively. Grasshoppers also gnaw their leaves, and Green Possums and pademelons are known to eat them. Even though the fruit is covered with toxic hairs, it is eaten by catbirds and others.

The plants' toxic juices and other defences may not eliminate leaf-eaters, but they do control them, limiting them to just a few species. If there were no poisonous chemicals, the plant kingdom would be at the mercy of the uncontrolled appetites of the leaf-eaters, and would soon be destroyed by them.

Male White Nymph

Female White Nymph

Lowland rainforest plants have large leaves like this Bernie's Tamarind.

The tropical rainforests are not an unending sea of green sameness. Differences in altitude, rainfall, soil, and drainage all create variations in the forests' structure. In Australia's wet tropics 13 main types are recognised. The classification system was devised by the plant ecologists Len Webb and Geoff Tracey who looked at the forests' structures, the interactions between species and their reactions to the physical environment. Their system applies to rainforests everywhere. Leaf size was an important criterion and was used to name the various types. Other characteristics used were: the tree strata, canopy height, plant species diversity (simple, mixed or complex), rainfall, soil fertility and drainage, altitude (which influences temperature and rainfall) and the presence or absence of rainforest characteristics such as tree buttresses, woody vines or lianes, cauliflory, strangler figs and epiphytes. To fully understand the system a few definitions are necessary.

LEAF SIZE

Three size classes are recognised in the wet tropics:

mesophyll: medium-leafed (*meso* means middle or medium and *phyll* means leaf) 127 mm or more in length
notophyll: (*noto* means southern and does not denote size) 76–127 mm in length
microphyll: small-leafed (*micro* means small) 25–76 mm in length

There are two other size classes: **megaphyll** (large-leafed), more than 127 mm long, including the really huge leaves of native bananas and gingers, and **nanophyll** (dwarf leafed), found on some plants on high, exposed mountain ridges. Neither form is sufficiently dominant to give its name to a rainforest type.

VINES

Vines, which include the thick, woody **lianes**, are an essential and prominent part of the rainforest. The terms **vine forest** and **vine thicket** do not indicate that the type is solely or even predominantly made up of vines, but rather that they are a conspicuous feature.

EMERGENTS

These are large trees whose crowns project well above the general level of the forest canopy.

ALTITUDE

Lowlands	less than 40 m
Foothills	40–400 m
Uplands	400–800 m
Highlands	800–1600 m

RAINFALL

Very wet	more than 3000 mm
Wet	2000–3000 mm
Cloudy wet	2000–3000 mm plus mist
Moist	1600–2000 mm
Cloudy moist	1600–2000 mm plus mist
Dry	1300–1600 mm

« Leaves of the cunjevoi

Swampy lowland rainforest in Daintree National Park

No.	Rainforest Type Name	Canopy Height	Special Features	Sub Type	Special Characteristics	Altitude	Rainfall	Soil, Parent Rock, Drainage	Where Found
1	Complex Mesophyll Vine Forest	uneven, 20-55 m occasional emergents to 65 m; many strata	buttresses well developed; woody vines and epiphytes prominent at all levels; most complex of all rainforests	1A	optimum rainforest in Australia	lowlands and foothills	very wet, and wet	alluvial basalt volcanics	Wooroonooran NP Mossman Gorge NP Daintree NP
				1B	gradual reduction in leaf size; less diversity; canopy higher than 1A	uplands	very wet, and wet, cloudy	very fertile basalt	eastern and south-eastern edges of Atherton Tableland
				1C	a few deciduous trees; epiphytes fewer	lowlands	moist and dry	river alluvial	along rivers in drier areas
2	Mesophyll Vine Forest	about 30 m	fewer trees with buttresses; fewer vines; fewer epiphytes on tree trunks	2A	cauliflory rare; strangler figs only occasional	lowlands and foothills	very wet, and wet	granite and metamorphics	rainforests below 400 m on soils of low fertility
				2B	wind shearing of canopy by trade winds; cyclone damage leading to uneven canopy and profuse growth of vines; epiphytes fewer	lowlands	very wet, and wet	beach sand	small patches behind beaches; Daintree NP and other coastal reserves
3	Mesophyll Vine Forest with Dominant Palms	10-20 m emergents to 36 m	composed mostly of palms with occasional broad-leafed emergents; buttresses, stilt roots common; lianes and epiphytes abundant; ground layer often dense	3A	dominant tree is Alexandra Palm	lowlands	very wet	alluvial and basalt; swampy	Only tiny patches remain at the mouth of Russell and Mulgrave Rivers and near Innisfail.
				3B	dominant tree is Fan Palm	lowlands	very wet	alluvial, granite and metamorphics; swampy	Tully-Mission Beach area; Daintree NP
4	Semi-deciduous Mesophyll Vine Forest	even, 25-32 m deciduous emergents to 36 m	buttressed trees common; buttresses large; cauliflorous trees and strangler figs only occasional; deciduous trees numerous; lianes common; epiphytes abound only in moist, sheltered pockets.	none		lowland and foothills	moist and dry	granite and basalt	between Bloomfield River and Cooktown
5	Complex Notophyll Vine Forest	uneven, 20-45 m many strata	tree buttresses common; large vines and epiphytes conspicuous; trees have great depth to their crowns	5A	deciduous trees rare; only occasional emergents; ferns, lianes, epiphytes prominent	highlands	cloudy wet	basalt and basic volcanics	Evelyn Tableland at southern end of Atherton Tableland
				5B	many trees semi-evergreen, ie, lose large proportion of leaves during dry spells; epiphytes prominent only in tree crowns	lowlands foothills and uplands	moist and dry	basalt	small patches at Wongabel, Yungaburra and Tolga is all that remains

No.	Rainforest Type Name	Canopy Height	Special Features	Sub Type	Special Characteristics	Altitude	Rainfall	Soil, Parent Rock, Drainage	Where Found
6	Complex Notophyll Vine Forest with Emergent Queensland Kauris	12-20 m emergents to 35 m	tree buttresses common; some deciduous species; heavy leaf fall during dry months; vines prominent; epiphytic ferns and orchids only in canopy	none		foothills and uplands	moist	granites and metamorphics	edge of main rainforest areas in north and west
7	Notophyll Vine Forest with Emergent Wattles	10-15 m in single stratum emergents to 30 m	buttressed trees and deciduous species rare or absent; cauliflory only on certain figs; woody vines and epiphytic ferns and orchids common in some places	none		lowland and foothills	moist and dry	granites, metamorphics and beach sands	sandy beaches along drier coast (Cook Highway) and some islands
8	Simple Notophyll Vine Forest – often with Bull Kauris	even, 24-33 m emergents to 45 m	buttressed trees, woody vines and deciduous species rare; wiry and thin vines common; epiphytes only on upper tree branches; groves of tree palms in gullies; tree ferns common	none		uplands and highlands	cloudy wet, and moist	granites, metamorphics and acid volcanics	most extensive mountain forest type on mainly granitic ranges from Ingham to Black Mountain at 400-1000 m altitude
9	Simple Microphyll Vine-Fern Forest – often with Mountain Kauris	even, 20-25 m emergent kauris to 35 m only two tree strata	buttressed trees, cauliflory and strangler figs rare or absent; epiphytic mosses, ferns and orchids common at all levels; large woody vines rare; slender, wiry vines common in patches; tree palms and tree ferns abundant; dense ground layer.	none		highlands	cloudy wet	granites	800-1300 m on mountains between Mt Bartle Frere and Mt Pieter Botte
10	Simple Microphyll Vine-Fern Thicket	10-12 m emergents to 15 m mostly two distinct strata	wind shearing of canopy; buttressed trees and cauliflory absent; vines sparse and wiry; ground cover of ferns including tree-ferns; epiphytic mosses and small orchids and ferns common	none		highlands	cloudy wet	granites	mostly above 1200 m on larger mountains
11	Deciduous Microphyll Vine Thicket	uneven 3-5 m emergents to 10 m	many deciduous trees; vines common including large woody species; many thorny shrubs and vines; fig trees conspicuous; epiphytic ferns and orchids common, low in trees; ground species die back during dry times	none		lowlands and foothills	dry	granites metamorphics	rocky outcrops and coastal headlands
12	Vine Forest with Wattles	uneven 20-30 m wattle emergents	different stages of succession after disturbance – logging, fire, cyclones	12A to 12D	sub-type is determined by which species of wattle dominates	lowlands to highlands	very wet, wet, and cloudy wet	granites and metamorphics	coastal flats and hills whose forests have been disturbed
13	Vine Forest with Eucalypts and Wattles	uneven 10-25 m emergent eucalypts to 36 m or even 55 m in gullies	different stages of succession after logging, fire, cyclones	13A to 13F	sub-type is determined by which species of eucalypt, wattle, box or turpentine dominates	lowlands to highlands	very wet, wet, cloudy wet and moist	mostly granite and metamorphics derived soils	lowlands to mountains often at edges of rainforest affected by fire

Raindrops on the flowers of a White Hazelwood

INTO THE RAINFORESTS

"... we can only understand the forests if we accept them for what they are. No one can improve an undisturbed rainforest. It is a culmination point ... as precious, worthy and sacred as any in the universe as we know it."

MARIUS JACOBS IN "THE TROPICAL RAINFOREST: A FIRST ENCOUNTER", 1988.

After a prolonged dry spell towards the end of December, low, dark clouds roll in from the northwest. They are so low that their ragged undersides drag over the ridge tops. Soon the sun is obscured and the light changes to a shadowless grey. The first heavy drops of rain hit the leaves. Faster and faster the drops fall until their drumming on the foliage produces a roar that drowns out all other sound. The monsoon has arrived.

For days it rains, sometimes in a light drizzle, sometimes in downpours so heavy you can see only a few metres ahead of you. The first day's rain is absorbed by the parched soil, but then run-off gathers in the gullies. Springs that had dried are gushing again. The continuing rain hisses and splashes in pools and swelling streams. Waterfalls thunder and fill their ravines with clouds of spray.

In the forest, rivulets trickle down tree trunks and large drops roll down the leaves. All of it is absorbed by the leaf-litter, now soft and springy, where before it had been hard and crackling. No birds sing or move about. Insects shelter under leaves or creep into crevices. Musky Rat-kangaroos remain curled up in their nests. Tree kangaroos sit huddled in tree forks, their head tucked in. Platypus stay in their burrows. Giant earthworms of a strange, blue colour and half a metre or more in length are flushed from their underground tunnels and crawl awkwardly among the fallen leaves. Only the frogs rejoice, and at night they gather around ponds to call and lay their eggs. Fallen logs soak up the water like sponges, encouraging the fungi to grow. Seeds, stored in the ground, swell and germinate. The densely-packed underground network of plant roots probes the soft soil for moisture and dissolved nutrients.

Rain, rain, rain. Rain from monsoon convergences; rain from violent cyclones; rain from black storm clouds; rain, benevolent and gentle from grey blankets borne on the tradewinds; rain in fleeting sun-showers. Whatever its source, the rain eventually stops: the sun re-emerges. It sparkles on the dripping foliage. Animals come out of hiding.

Birds sing with renewed vitality. A Lewin's Honeyeater bathes by flying into raindrop-laden leaves. A Brown Pigeon rises steeply into the air then glides down to a treetop in a joyous aerobatics display. A male Brush Turkey, his yellow wattle almost touching the ground, rises on tiptoe and exuberantly beats his wings. Insects buzz and zip through the foliage. Snakes uncoil themselves and lie in patches of warming sun. The colours of butterflies once again flash among the leaves.

Rain and sun are the two vital forces that create the tropical evergreen forests, that make this boundless life possible.

This part of the book deals with the animal and plant life of four broad categories of rainforest: lowland, upland, mountain top and that along the rainforest edges.

While each of the divisions has species restricted to it, there is a certain amount of overlap between them. Flying-foxes, for example, occur not only in the lowlands, but also at quite high altitudes. Many kinds of plants, too, have extensive distributions. Unless specifically stated, plants and animals are not necessarily restricted to the regions in which they are depicted. Despite having some species in common, each type of rainforest has its own special character.

A male Orange-eyed Tree Frog singing

The sun filters through tree fern fronds.

A Ulysses Butterfly shelters from the rain.

« A sun shower in upland rainforest

IN THE LOWLANDS

Lowland rainforests grow on the coastal plains to an altitude of 40 m. Up until recent times, large areas of swamp existed close to the sea front where Fan Palms and Alexandra Palms grew in almost pure stands. In places where the soil was well drained and fertile grew the wet tropics' tallest forests. Here trees and other plants had the largest, softest leaves, attained their greatest size, and were linked together in the most complex associations. Or at least they would have if they had been sheltered from the destructive force of the cyclones. These spiralling gales can knock down the largest trees and blast open the forest canopy, leaving the way open for the invasion of smothering growths of vines. In these places, the trees never reach their full potential size.

That is how things were 200 years ago. Very little remains of these types of forests today — they have been cut down to make way for people

Lowland rainforest in Mossman Gorge

A large fig tree in lowland forest

A Grey Satinash

« Black Palms against misty hills (photo: Belinda Wright)

Slender tree ferns in lowland rainforest

and their activities. Only at McNamee Creek and Downey Creek, west of Innisfail, do small patches of sheltered lowland rainforest that is growing on fertile soil remain. They have been logged and it will take several centuries before they are once again primary forests. A few tiny patches of palm

A stag beetle

swamp survive. The only substantial areas of lowland rainforest remaining are in the Cape Tribulation region in the Daintree National Park. But these suffer from cyclone damage and grow on poorer soils.

As far as the animal life is concerned, the lowlands are the realm of insects and

spiders. Bird and mammal life is also rich but is less varied than on the tablelands. Frogs are more numerous on the coastal plains, while reptiles have similar numbers to those on the higher altitudes. Streams, once they reach the plain, lose much of their force. Colourful freshwater fish abound in their wide pools.

The profusion of the insects and the lushness of the plants characterise the lowland rainforest.

MANGROVE FORESTS

A Saltwater Crocodile resting on a mud bank (photo: Belinda Wright)

Mangrove trees are restricted to the inter-tidal zone in river and creek estuaries. The forests they form are unlike any other. High rainfall is of little or no consequence in their development. In the wet tropics, mangroves grade into rainforest wherever estuaries and beaches have been left undisturbed. The many species of mangrove gain their nourishment from tidal areas of mud where they have adapted to being flooded by saltwater twice every 24 hours. There is no undergrowth. When the forest floor, made up entirely of mud, is exposed at low tide, crabs, mudskippers, molluscs and other saltwater denizens crawl and scuttle among the tree roots. Above the high tide mark, however, rainforest elements may take hold. Epiphytic orchids and ferns crowd tree limbs and trunks. Close to the rainforest, vines wind and twist themselves into the mangrove trees. Weaver ants hunt and golden orb-weaving spiders set their webs. The voices of Black Butcherbirds, Rose-crowned Pigeons, Yellow-spotted Honeyeaters and other rainforest birds are raised in the mangroves.

Many other species are mangrove specialists — warblers, kingfishers, rails, flycatchers, whistlers and other birds, as well as mangrove goannas and snakes.

The wet tropics' largest predator, the Saltwater Crocodile, cruises the estuaries and inlets and basks on mud banks. The region's only truly dangerous animal, this reptile can grow to more than seven metres in length, but rarely reaches such gigantic proportions. However, they are all efficient predators and even crocodiles three or four metres long can be dangerous to humans.

The massive jaws of a Saltwater Crocodile

A mangrove tree

« Saltwater Crocodile

The estuary of Emmagen Creek in Daintree National Park, prime crocodile habitat

PALM SWAMPS

Alexandra Palms

Alexandra Palm fruits

Also waterlogged, but only during the wet season, is another beguiling forest of singular character. Its trees are not mangroves, but palms, and the water they stand in is not salt, but fresh. Among the tall palms there can be a dense, green undergrowth of sedges, ferns, and pandans. On a windy, sunny morning, when the song of shrike-thrushes and the ooms and coos of fruit pigeons resound, and the dew drips loudly on the giant fronds, palm forests

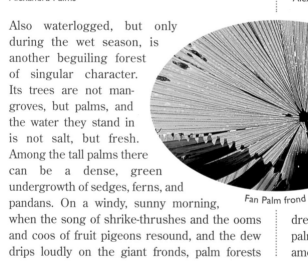

Fan Palm frond

can seem a little eerie. The long-handled fronds of the fan palms rub together, making strange creaking sounds. The early sun makes shifting patterns of green and yellow. Figbirds, pigeons, koels and other birds come to eat the fruit of the Alexandra Palm that grows in enormous bunches, hanging down like scarlet dreadlocks. A Green Tree Snake may glide from palm to pandanus, or a lace monitor may stride among the fallen fronds.

Fan Palms

« Fruit of the Alexandra Palm

In a Fan Palm swamp

Fallen Fan Palm fronds

Base of a Black Palm surrounded by its fallen fruit

Green Tree Snake

A few other species — paperbarks, satinashes, and walnuts — grow as isolated trees among the dense stands of palms. These often large trees are heavily laden with orchids, ferns, strangler figs, and the clawing, hooked wait-a-whiles, which are also palms. The trunks of the palms are too smooth and straight to provide a foothold for those opportunist plants.

Palms are among the most ancient flowering plants. Some, like the wait-a-whiles, have hardly changed from their earliest ancestral forms. Walking through these primeval palm swamps, it is possible to experience the long, unbroken continuity of the wet tropics' rainforests.

ALONG A STREAM

Pools in Gap Creek and other lowland streams abound with fish.

To a visitor seated on a large, moss-covered boulder, a pool in a rainforest stream can be an extraordinarily peaceful place. The light, filtering through the crowns of trees arching over the creek, creates a green calmness. Water running over stones whispers softly. Yellow Orioles call lazily in bubbly notes: "choom cha-loom". Turtles crawl onto rocks to rest or to sun them-selves. Brightly coloured fish rise languidly to falling leaves that drift down to the crystal-clear water.

Banded Rainbowfish

But for the animals here, life is as hazardous and as much of a struggle as anywhere else. An Azure Kingfisher dashes into the water and emerges with a fish in its dagger-like beak. A fish leaps out of the water and grabs a dragonfly in mid-air. Another dragonfly, a species that is the largest in the world, zips across a pool at a speed almost too fast for the eye to follow, and captures a blue-banded eggfly. Between the rocks, a water snake catches a small frog, which cries pitifully.

Snakehead Gudgeon

Banded Rainbowfish

« *Petalura ingentissima*, the world's largest dragonfly

Along the lower reaches of many rivers and major creeks grows a distinctive, smooth-barked tree — the river box (above and left). Growing right on the water's edge, its roots grip the bank to brace it against the tearing and gouging water during floods. They mature into rugged, tortured-looking trees.

White-lipped Tree Frog

During exceptionally heavy rain, such as that which usually accompanies a cyclone, most streams overflow and create broad pools, often choked with aquatic grasses. On the night after the first flood of the season, enormous numbers of frogs of many species gather at the overflowing ponds to spawn. The males inflate themselves and call with such force that it seems they must burst. Each species has its own particular call and its own calling position relative to the water. In this way males attract only females of their own species. The frog chorus on that first night is one of unquenchable passion.

Top left: A pair of Dainty Tree Frogs ready to spawn
Centre left: A Red Tree Frog calling

INSECTS

Caterpillar of a fruit-sucking moth

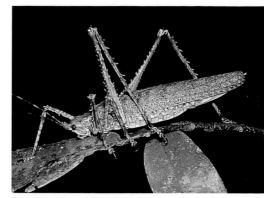
Spiny Long-horned Grasshopper (photo: Belinda Wright)

The first substantial storm rain of the season, though not necessarily a flood, brings out hordes of insects, especially moths and beetles. These have been dormant as pupae or nymphs during the cooler and drier months, and the storm is their signal to break out and become mature insects. The warmer weather and rain invigorate the plants, providing a fresh supply of food for a new generation of insects. The insects display or otherwise attract their mates. Females lay their eggs, which soon hatch into larvae that begin to gnaw at the forest.

The numbers of individual insects and the variety of species defy description. Among the moths alone there are thousands of undescribed species. The air is filled with the flapping wings of giant moths, loudly buzzing beetles, as well as those of tiny bugs and praying mantises.

Pink-spotted Longicorn Beetle

Praying mantis devouring a katydid

Top and above: Long-legged Longicorn Beetle

Rhinoceros Beetle

« *Top to bottom:* Bush Cricket in defence posture; Praying Mantis; moths are among the most numerous insects in the rainforest

OTHER NIGHTLIFE

Boobook Owl

Ghost Bat

The insects are a bonanza for many night predators. Owls and the larger insect-eating bats catch moths, beetles, crickets, long-horned grasshoppers, mantids and others. Tiny bats flutter through the forest in pursuit of small, even minute, flying insects such as mosquitoes. Not all the nocturnal species are hunters. Red-legged Pademelons browse on the leaves of seedling trees and feed on fallen fruit. Tube-nosed Bats and the much larger flying-foxes search the forest for fruiting trees. Once they find a tree to their liking, they will return to it night after night, until the fruit crop is consumed.

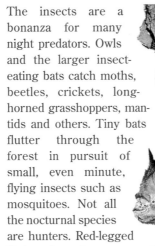
Diadem Bat

Tube-nosed Bat

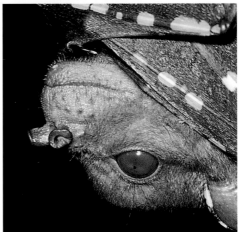
Tube-nosed Bat in close-up

Red-legged Pademelon, a small rainforest wallaby

Spectacled Flying-fox

FLYING-FOX CAMP

Little Red Flying-foxes take to the air from their daytime roost.

Well before first light, the flying-foxes leave their feeding trees and fly back to their daytime roosts or camps. The journey can be long, as much as 40 km, and may take well over an hour. At daybreak, however, most bats are in their camp, usually in a flat area of rainforest near water. Here they crowd together in their thousands, sometimes in hundreds of thousands, and try to sleep. But there is a great deal of screeching and noisy bickering all day long. When it becomes hot, the bats fan themselves with one of their huge wings. Sleep is mostly fitful. At nightfall they return to their favourite food trees or look for new ones. It seems they find them through their keen sense of smell.

Spectacled Flying-fox and young

« Little Red Flying-foxes

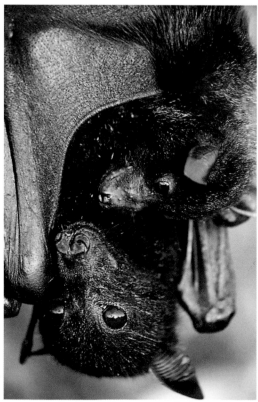

Black Flying-fox and young (photo: Belinda Wright)

Spectacled Flying-fox

Little Red Flying-fox

Spectacled Flying-foxes resting in their roosts

SNAKES OF THE NIGHT

Carpet Python swallowing a flying-fox (photo: Belinda Wright)

Carpet Python

Amethyst Python, Australia's largest snake (photo: Belinda Wright)

« Sloughed skin of a Brown Tree Snake

Pythons are sometimes seen during the day, sliding slowly through the undergrowth or warming themselves in a patch of sunlight. Brown Tree Snakes, however, do not venture out in broad daylight; they remain coiled in tree hollows or other secluded places. At night they wend their way through branches and leaves, stalking sleeping birds or crawling towards rodents engrossed in their search for food.

The Amethyst Python and the Carpet Python also hunt at night. They seek out warm-blooded animals, including flying-foxes. The pythons sense the heat radiated by birds and mammals with special receptors in pits on their lower lips. They can detect their prey even in total darkness. Once within range of that prey, they strike and wrap their muscular coils tightly around it, and squeeze it to death. Pythons are non-venomous and are among the largest of snakes. An Amethyst Python has been recorded at over eight metres in length, but this is exceptional. On average they are between three and four metres long.

Carpet Python. The constantly flicking tongue is a sense organ.

A Brown Tree Snake poised to strike

THE FIG TREES

Section through a Banana Fig showing the fig wasps

Fig trees, especially the stranglers, form one of the most prominent elements of the tropical rainforests. These trees grow to be among the largest and can be found in all but the highest altitude forests. However, they seem to reach their greatest development in the lowlands and foothills.

About 40 species of fig are found in the wet tropics. Their mature fruit may be green or red, purple or yellow, pink or dark brown. The fruit vary in size from half a centimetre in diameter, to the 7 cm long Banana Fig. But whatever their

Both kinds of fig wasp are clearly visible.

colour or size, the mature fruit, the figs, have one thing in common: they began as a container of the flowers, several hundred of them, which develop *inside* the fig. At that stage it is the inflorescence.

The most remarkable thing about the fig's inflorescence is its intimate partnership with the insects that pollinate it. The tiny gall wasp enters the inflorescence when it is still green and hard, through an opening at the top. This opening is so tight that when the female wasp pushes through, her wings are torn off. The first flowers she squeezes past are male, but they have not yet matured, and carry no pollen. She moves further into the hollow inflorescence lined with female flowers, and dusts them with the pollen that she has brought with her from the fig in which she herself grew up. She now lays her eggs in the small female flowers and dies soon after. The eggs hatch and the larvae develop rapidly, eating some of the flowers. The male wasps are the first to emerge, looking nothing like a wasp, having neither wings nor eyes. Yet they can detect the females and mate with them. Before they die, the males perform one other duty — they enlarge the original entrance to a wider tunnel, so that the females can exit without losing their wings.

The fig *Ficus virgata*

« The trunk of a Rusty Fig, a species of strangler

Banana Fig

While the larvae grew inside the fig, the male flowers developed and now carry their pollen. The female wasps, as they squeeze past, are dusted with this pollen and will carry it to another green fig, where they in turn will lay their eggs.

Another kind of gall wasp takes a short cut in this whole process. The female does not squeeze into the green fig. Instead, she inserts her long ovipositor (an appendage for placing eggs) through the fig's entrance and lays her eggs deep inside. She is of no use to the fig, for she carries no pollen to cross-fertilise the flowers.

Once the wasps have left or died, the figs ripen into fruit. The flowers have grown to seeds. The figs take on a bright colour, and become soft and succulent. They are now one of the most important trees for the fruit-eating birds and mammals. Without the figs many of them could not survive.

Banana Figs at different stages of ripeness

THE FIG-EATERS

While fruit can sometimes be abundant in the rainforest, there are seasons, such as the drier months, when it is scarce. Also, for reasons yet unknown, there are years when trees put on little or no fruit. These are times of real hardship for such exclusive fruit-eaters as the fruit pigeons, and even for flying-foxes, cassowaries and others who supplement their diet with other food. However, figs are not strictly seasonal, and they fruit most years. There is always a fig tree in fruit somewhere in the forest and they sustain the fruit-eaters during hard times.

A giant fig tree in fruit is one of the great spectacles of the rainforest. If you stand quietly at some vantage point, you will see a constant stream of birds feeding on the fruit. The birds range in size from the huge Channel-billed Cuckoo to the tiny silvereye — so small that it half disappears inside the fruit it is feeding on. At night, flying-foxes eat the fruit, and squabble over the feeding territories they have staked out for themselves.

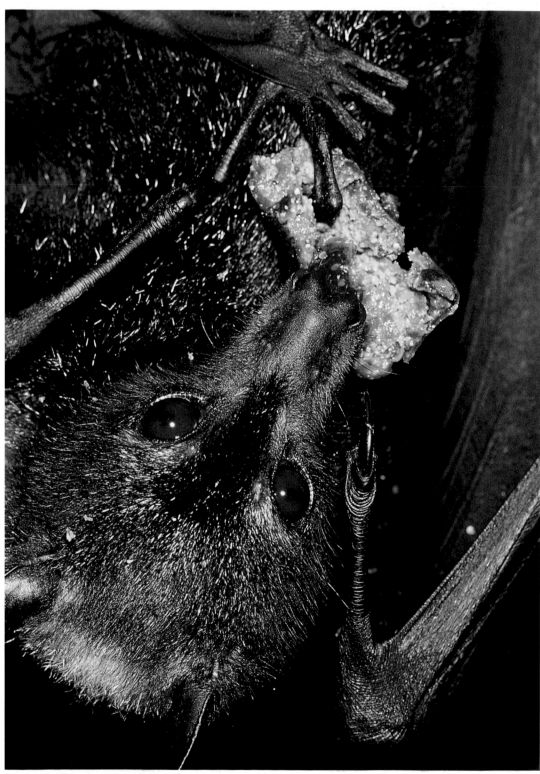

A Spectacled Flying-fox eating a Watkin's Fig

« Cluster Figs appear on the tree's trunk and main branches.

Cluster Figs

A Wompoo Pigeon can swallow large fruit.

Male Figbird singing

The Musky Rat-kangaroo eats fallen fruit, including figs. (photo: Belinda Wright)

Female Figbird on the nest

INSECT DAYS

Australian Rustic

Union Jacks

Hot, humid days, such as those you might find in the middle of the wet season, are the days that you realise that the lowlands are the lands of insects — a world of movement and colour. The best place to observe this world is where an opening in the forest canopy allows a broad shaft of sunlight to strike the lush

Stag beetle

undergrowth. Butterflies and day-flying moths flit in and out of the sun. Equally brilliant beetles and bugs suck the nectar from flowers or the juice from leaf stems. A closer look will reveal other intriguing details, such as stick insects and katydids so well camouflaged you notice them only when they move.

Stick insect showing lichen-like camouflage

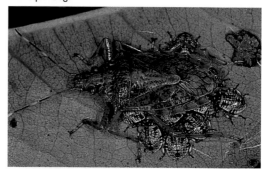
Harlequin Bugs

Katydid with wings resembling leaves

A shield bug with young

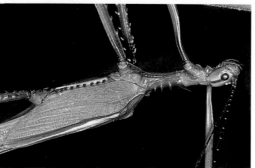
Euodia Stick Insect

« Detail of the wing of a Union Jack butterfly

Shield bugs sucking sap from a tree branch

The Jumping Spider, *Mopsus mormon*

The cornucopia of food-on-the-wing that the insects provide does not go unexploited. Spiders, especially, lie in ambush or set their snares across the insects' flightpaths.

Red Spined Spider

The Turret Spider, *Dolophones turrigera*

A jumping spider has caught a fly.

Golden Orb-weaving Spider with Ulysses Butterfly

Striped Spined Spider with fly

OTHER INSECT PREDATORS

Shiny-skinned lizards dash in and out of the hot sun to catch flies, beetles and others. Small birds search the foliage minutely for insects and spiders, and carry them off to feed their nestlings. Other birds — such as the scrubfowl, Brush Turkeys and chowchillas — rake over the leaf-litter for cockroaches, beetles and springtails.

Top to bottom, left to right: Brush Turkey; Limbless Snake-toothed Skink; Scrubfowl; Pink Tongue Skink; a male Lovely Wren feeds his young on insects; Spectacled Flycatcher; Litter Rainbow-skink

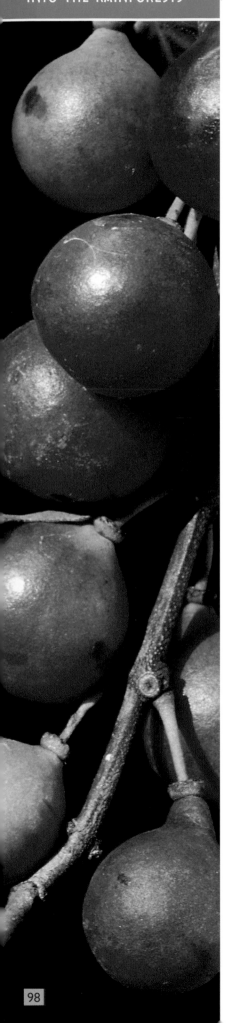

CASSOWARIES

When it is cold or wet the young Southern Cassowary chicks shelter under their father.

When fruits are plentiful, mostly in the warmer, wetter months, they shine in brilliant colours among the green foliage, and lie like scattered bright jewels on the dull-brown carpet of the forest floor. At about this time, the large green eggs of some of the cassowaries may hatch, though their nesting is not strictly seasonal. The downy young are patterned in stripes of light and dark brown. The male cassowary alone incubates the eggs, usually 3 to 5 in a clutch. During the 48- to 50-day incubation period, he never leaves the nest.

The male also raises the chicks on his own. Being very protective of them, he chases off any potential predators — goannas, dingos, feral pigs and dogs. He leads the young to fallen fruit and even breaks up the larger ones for them with his strong beak. When the weather is wet and cold, he squats down so that the young can shelter under him.

All this care and attention changes to aggression when the young are about a year old. By then, the chicks have changed to brown plumage and are about three-quarters the size of their parent. This same parent now chases the yearling vigorously, kicking at it and butting it with his chest. Eventually he banishes his offspring from his territory. He is ready to be courted by the female again.

The male cassowary looks after the chicks on his own.

« Lolly Berries – fruits of a vine eaten by cassowaries and other birds

The male picks leeches off his young.

Cassowary Plum

At about one year old this chick is newly independent.

Male cassowary

ON THE TABLELANDS

Nandroya Falls

Most of the great rainforests that remain in the wet tropics grow in the foothills and on the tablelands between 40 and 800 m in altitude. All the hill forests from Paluma to Black Mountain are of this kind. The most extensive forests are in the Lumholtz, Wooroonooran and Daintree National Parks and the state forests in the Mt Lewis, Mt Carbine and the Mt Windsor Tableland areas.

The word "medium" seems most applicable to these forests. While not quite as lush as those of the coastal plains, they are not as constrained by the cold and constant wind as those of the mountain tops.

At these medium altitudes, there are more species, as well as individuals, of birds and mammals. Insects and frogs, while still abundant, are less numerous than in the warmer lowlands. Fishes, unable to ascend the waterfalls that cascade down the escarpment, are poorly represented.

Trees, where they are protected from the cyclones and the constant blast of the tradewinds, grow to an enormous size. The heavy rains collect in fast-flowing streams that cut ravines through the ranges, and plunge down the escarpment in spectacular waterfalls.

The uplands are places of giant trees, tall waterfalls, possums, tree kangaroos and rainforest wilderness filled with the songs of birds.

A Grey Fantail on its nest

Green Ringtail Possum with young

« A river bank smothered in several species of fern

Lemuroid Ringtail Possum and young

THE WARMTH OF SPRING

On the tablelands, the seasons are more pronounced than on the lowlands. Winter is cool. With spring's first warmth, orchids come out in flower. As the season progresses and banishes the cool weather altogether, many kinds of insects emerge. Among them are special upland species, including a very large bull ant which can inflict a severely painful sting. This primitive and ancient species survives only at higher altitudes, because in the lowlands it has been displaced by more aggressive, modern ants. The spring warmth encourages the larvae of

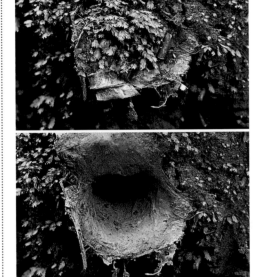

Weevil of the genus *Leptops*

Mueller's Stag Beetles to change into pupae and eventually into large, shiny beetles. Rainforest dragons, snakes and other reptiles come out to sun themselves. But it is not until the heat of summer that the cicadas, such as the Green Baron, make the air vibrate with their shrill, penetrating sounds.

Two Red Carabeen trees with their root systems fused

A trapdoor spider's burrow with its lid closed and open

This spider of the genus *Cataxia*, made the burrow.

Giant Climbing Orchid

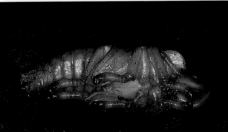

Mueller's Stag Beetle: larva, pupa and male adult

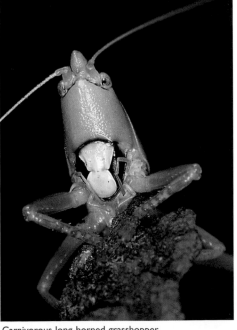

Small-eyed Snake

Carnivorous long-horned grasshopper

FORESTS OF BIRDS

Buttresses of a 500-year-old Red Cedar

Male Golden Whistler

Macleay's Honeyeater

« Wing feathers of the Green-winged Pigeon

The first thing you notice as you enter one of the tablelands' great unlogged forests, is the massive size of some of the trees — a Red Cedar, perhaps, or a Grey Satinash. The ground cover is more sparse in such a place and it is easier to walk about. The air is cooler and less oppressive than on the lowlands. Mosquitoes are mostly absent. There are no weaver ants. The forest at sunrise reverberates with an astonishing chorus of birdsong — songs of great variety, sung by strong voices. The strongest voices and most vigorous songs belong to the chowchillas or Northern Logrunners. Chowchillas live in groups of from three to eight birds, and every morning, especially in spring, each group engages its neighbours in duels of song — testing and demarcating their territorial boundaries. The chowchilla is not a large bird, about 27 cm in overall length including its tail, but its voice is prodigious. At close quarters its call is so loud it can be painful to the human ear.

Besides the voices of chowchillas, those of shrike-thrushes, whipbirds, riflebirds, Tooth-billed Bowerbirds, King Parrots, flycatchers and others resound through the vaulted forest. Other, softer, voices of scrubwrens, robins, honeyeaters, fantails, silvereyes and many more whisper in the undergrowth. Alert to the songsters' every move, the Grey Goshawk watches for an opportunity to strike one of them down.

Grey Goshawk

King Parrots

About 16 species of birds are restricted to the higher altitude rainforests, and another eight or so are mostly found there, only occasionally going down to the lowlands. Among them are many of the species unique to the wet tropics, such as the Golden and Tooth-billed Bowerbirds, the Atherton Scrubwren, the fernwren and the Grey-headed Robin. The lowlands too have their own birds, including such beautiful species as the White-tailed Kingfisher, the Lovely Wren and the Metallic Starling. Nevertheless, it is the higher altitude forests that give the impression of being forests of birds.

Male King Parrot

Eastern Whipbird

Grey-headed Robin

Victoria's Riflebird nest with a snake skin woven into it

Male Victoria's Riflebird

A male Victoria's Riflebird displays to the pale brown female.

103

CRATER LAKES

Lake Barrine

Lakes Barrine, Eacham and Euramoo were formed by volcanic explosions on the Atherton Tableland about 95 000 years ago. Now they are surrounded by rainforest. Included are patches of forest, growing on the basalt-derived soils, which are the most complex outside those of the lowlands. These forests are home to giant trees, including Red Cedars, kauris, satinashes and especially a species of strangler fig variously called Australian Banyan, Deciduous Fig, White Fig and,

Pencil Orchid

in one particular form, Curtain Fig. The largest of these figs grow along the lakes' edges, where they lean far out across the water. On their landward side, the figs are anchored by thick, cable-like aerial roots. On the lake side, their heavy horizontal limbs are supported by a phalanx of prop roots. Turtles rest on them and waterdragons chase each other through the maze of branches. Bunches of Pencil Orchids grip the bark with their roots and sway in the breeze like wind chimes.

A White Fig leans out over the waters of Lake Barrine.

« Lake Euramoo

Pelicans and other birds at Lake Barrine

Early morning on Lake Barrine

The lakes are encircled by loose rock slopes, about 50 m high, that were deposited during the volcanic explosion. No creeks flow into the lakes; their water supply comes from the run-off of the crater walls. The deep water is crystal clear and it is possible to see numerous fish swimming around the edges. In Lake Eacham, there were originally three native fishes, the Fly-specked Hardyhead, the Trout Gudgeon and the Lake Eacham Rainbowfish. Other species were introduced from surrounding rivers. As a result, the Eacham Rainbowfish disappeared from the lake. Efforts to re-introduce it have so far failed, and it survives in only a few other places.

The lakes' clear water is poor in animal and plant nutrients. Only a few special plants, waterlilies and sedges mostly, grow in the shallow bays, yet this is sufficient to maintain a small population of waterbirds.

Top, left to right: Wandering Whistling-duck; Dusky Moorhen
Bottom, left to right: White-eyed Duck; Eastern Water-skink

AT NIGHT

Young Lumholtz's Tree-kangaroo

At dusk, when it is almost dark inside the rainforest, a species of bright-green cicada with red eyes begins to sing. For about 15 minutes its song pierces the air at 120 decibels. Then suddenly it stops. At about the same time, the rainforest possums emerge from their dens in hollow trees where they have slept during the day. The cicada is known as the Possum Alarm. Its other name is the Northern Greengrocer. Eight species of possum are busy feeding during the night, and all but one feed on leaves, flowers and fruit. That species specialises in pulling apart rotting wood with its teeth and elongated fingers. The Striped Possum feeds on cockroaches, beetles, their grubs, and other invertebrates it extracts from the soft, spongy, decaying wood.

Possum Alarm cicada

Another species, the Green Ringtail Possum, does not sleep in a tree hollow. It spends most of the day curled up on a tree branch or vine — a green ball of fur in the green foliage.

Tree-kangaroos also roost out in the open, even during the heaviest rain. Two species are found in Australia. Bennett's Tree-kangaroo lives in the lowland and tableland rainforests, between the Daintree River and the area close to Black Mountain. Lumholtz's Tree-kangaroo lives in the uplands, between Kirrama and Mount Spurgeon. Tree-kangaroos are ungainly animals that lack the fluid grace of the ringtail possums.

Face of the White-kneed Weta

Possum Alarm cicada or Northern Greengrocer

« The upland rainforest is a busy place at night. (photo: Belinda Wright)

Green Ringtail Possum eating fig leaves and in sleeping posture

Rufous Owl

They are awkward climbers, shuffling along horizontal branches, yet spend most of their time in the treetops. When they do want to descend a tree in a hurry, they simply leap down, even from heights of 20 m or more.

Large moths of many colours flutter through the forest at night. Strange kinds of crickets called wetas, some with prominent white "knees", leap over the forest floor. Moss-green frogs, with turquoise eyes, ambush insects along streams, while camouflaged geckoes stalk the tree trunks. Bulbous-eyed Brown Tree Snakes slide through the foliage in pursuit of sleeping birds and small rodents. Tableland rainforests are busy places at night.

White-kneed Weta

Herbert River Ringtail Possum

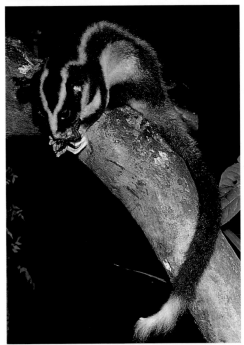

Striped Possum eating a bush cockroach

Coppery Brushtail Possum

Blue-banded Moth

Chameleon Gecko

Yellow Emperor Moth in threat display

Green-eyed Tree Frog

WATERFALLS

Wallaman Falls – a 279-metre drop

Tchupala Falls

Streams tumble down the mountainsides onto the tablelands, rush through narrow ravines and then crash down the escarpment in a series of waterfalls and rapids. Some of Australia's most imposing falls are found in the wet tropics. Wallaman Falls is the country's highest single-drop waterfall. When in full flood, Barron Falls is one of the most spectacular.

On the Atherton Tableland, a series of waterfalls runs down gorges such as Nandroya, Wallacher, and Tchupala Falls on Henrietta Creek in the Palmerston Section of Wooroonooran National Park.

Around the plunge pools at the bases of the falls, the forest and rocks are constantly wet and misty from the spray. In this dampness, mosses, filmy ferns and orchids thrive. Dragonflies and damselflies skim across the pools. In quiet backwaters birds come to drink and bathe.

Barron Falls in flood

« Nandroya Falls in Wooroonooran National Park

Zillie Falls

Top, left to right: Wallaman Falls; Elinjaa Falls; Wallaman Falls
Centre, left to right: Boea hygroscopica flowers during the wet season;
Red-browed Firetails bathing in a rock pool; *Boea hygroscopica*
Bottom, left to right: Filmy ferns; the orchid *Bulbophyllum schillerianum;*
mist-filled canyon below Barron Falls

IN THE MOUNTAINS

The summit of Mount Bartle Frere (photo: Andrew Dennis)

The summits of the mountains, rising above 800 m, are mysterious places. The wind-blasted trees are short but sturdy, and draped with trailing growths of mosses and lichens. Clumps of orchids adorn rocks and tree limbs. Wait-a-whiles and other vines are few. Gigantic strangler figs are also scarce. Some forests are open and easy to walk about in, while others have dense thickets of dwarf palms and other shrubs. The peaks are swathed in mist more often than not, and receive unimaginably heavy rain. They can be cold and windy, but on a sunny day no place is more invigorating.

Animal life at these altitudes is less varied, but remains prolific, especially among the birds. A few fish species are found in the streams, and on some peaks large freshwater crayfish live in bouldery pools. On all but the most exposed peaks live possums and tree kangaroos. The insect life is vastly different. Ants are few compared to the lowlands, where they dominate the insect fauna. This allows other insect groups to flourish such as the wingless carabid beetles and certain kinds of stag beetles. It is in the mountains that the Gondwana insects survive.

Highland rainforest

« Mist on mountain ridges

Mountain rainforest in the Mount Lewis region

The mountain wilderness regions of the wet tropics are among the least explored in Australia. These are wondrous places, usually wrapped in mist, where stunted forests crouch between granite outcrops.

Wingless carabid beetle, *Pamborus opacus*

The orchid *Dendrobium carri* grows in high altitude cloud forests.

AROUND THE SUMMITS

Along the north-west ridge of Mount Bartle Frere grows the highest altitude rainforest. (photo: Andrew Dennis)

The exposed summits are cool to cold, wind-swept and misty. Plants living there must be hardy. Their leaves are small to tiny, and often have a leathery texture. Soft, large leaves, such as are found on lowland plants, would soon be shredded and torn from their branches. Tree growth is slow. The Mountain Tea Tree, which is only found above 1100 m in the Mount Lewis region and on Mount Bellenden Ker, is believed to be among the most ancient of trees, some thousands of years old. Yet they are not massive.

Summit plants grow in dense thickets in the sheltered spaces among boulders, but the constant wind does not allow the plants to rise above them. Many of these plants have colourful and delicate flowers, like the native rhododendron and a dracophyllum. Epiphytic orchids also flower in these protected places.

Oak Orchid

Orchids and ferns on Mount Bartle Frere summit (photo: Andrew Dennis)

« The canopy of mountain forest on Mount Bellenden Ker (photo: Belinda Wright)

The tree with the pale trunk is the Mountain Tea Tree near the summit of Mount Bellenden Ker. (photo: Belinda Wright)

Australian Rhododendron

Australian Rhododendron

Buttercup Orchid with moths

The orchid Dendrobium adae

Dracophyllum flowers

The leaves of the Cherry Satinash are small.

Apricot Orchid

FORESTS OF STURDY TREES

The Spotted-tailed Quoll survives mostly in the highlands where it hunts possums and rodents. (photo: Ian Morris)

Immediately below the exposed summits grow dense forests. Their trees are not overly tall, but have thick and sturdy trunks. This, too, is a realm of specialised plants, like the Atherton Palm, which grows in thickets. When in season their brilliant red fruit hang down in long strings. The Buff Carabeen has bunches of orange-red fruit covered in rusty-coloured hairs. Christmas Orchids, so called because of the season of their flowering, grow where humus has accumulated among rocks or between logs. Upland beetles, like the wingless carabids, sprint over the leaf-litter at night in pursuit of snails, earthworms and even lizards. Should there be a sunny day, Red-bellied Black Snakes come out to bask in dapples of sunlight.

Fruit of Syzygium erythrodoxum

The Golden Bowerbird, unique to the higher altitudes of the wet tropics, and the Satin Bowerbird build their bowers in the highest forests. The Tooth-billed Bowerbird, another species unique to the region, builds its court on all but the highest ridges. The bowerbirds' strange and varied voices add to these forests' intriguing air of mystery.

In the northern mountains lives the Daintree Possum and you occasionally see Bennett's Tree-kangaroo there. The mountains also seem to be the last stronghold of the Spotted-tailed Quoll, a rare and agile hunter of possums and birds.

A male Golden Bowerbird tends his bower.

« Mountain rainforest

Bower of the Golden Bowerbird

Fruit of the Atherton Palm

Atherton Palm

Fruit of the Rusty Carabeen

MOUNTAIN STREAMS

The mountains are made of granite. Water, over millions of years, wears it down to a coarse, pale sand. Consequently, mountain streams, their spring water filtered to a crystal clarity, run over clean, sandy beds. The constantly moist atmosphere around the creeks ensures that the boulders in them and on their banks support green gardens of mosses and ferns.

Once these streams resounded, by day and night, with the calls of many species of frogs. Sadly, many voices have been stilled as the torrent frogs disappeared from the mountains.

Above: Lesueur's Frog
Left: A mountain stream
Below, left to right: Northern Barred Frog; Mount Lewis Crayfish; Robust Frog

AT THE EDGE OF THE RAINFOREST

Fruit of the Red Beech

Wherever the rainforest meets other habitats, there is a narrow zone where the two intermingle. In this area of interchange, be it along a beach, river, lake, eucalypt forest or artificial clearing, life is richly varied. Not only are there species from the two habitats, but there are also ones that specialise in living at this meeting place. Such birds as Metallic Starlings and sunbirds, for example, will feed inside the rainforest, but nest only at its edge. Along beaches, rivers and lakes, the trunks of trees lean outwards over the sand and water and almost grow horizontally. With the vines and shrubs they form a wall of vegetation from the topmost tree right to the ground. It appears as if the canopy has been tilted 90 degrees. The animals certainly seem to think so, for insects and birds usually seen skimming over the tree tops, here come down to within a metre of the ground. You can see butterflies sipping nectar from flowers and birds feeding on fruits at eye-level.

Whether along a beach at Cape Tribulation, or bordering a mountain forest of rose gums with glistening white trunks, the edge of the rainforest is a lively place of brightness and colour.

Blue Triangle Butterfly

« At Cape Tribulation

Cape Tribulation

ALONG THE BEACH

Beach Calophyllum

Where the rainforest meets the beach there is a wonderful mix of specialist trees and shrubs, and those of the regular lowland rainforest. In undisturbed places, like those around Cape Tribulation, the Beach Calophyllums are especially impressive. Their thick trunks and limbs reach as far out as possible towards the sea, to escape the shade of

Red Beech flower

the forest. The trees' roots also grow outwards, but are thwarted by the salt water, and must bend back at the high tide mark. In swampy places, huge paperbark trees grow in the rainforest.

Lush and colourful flowers abound. One of the largest orchids, the Golden Orchid, grows in clumps on exposed rocks and large tree branches.

Weeping Paperbarks

Red Beech flower

Golden Orchid

« *Top to bottom:* Flowers of Beach Calophyllum; fruit of Beach Barringtonia; flower of Beach Barringtonia

Rainforest along the beach

Cottonwood or Beach Hibiscus

Beach Stone Curlew

The weeping plants along the beach provide sheltered nesting places for such birds as the Beach Stone Curlew. White-breasted Sea-Eagles make their huge nests in tall paperbarks.

One of the most remarkable rainforest plants along the shore is the Matchbox Bean, a vine so large that it may entwine a dozen trees. The bean pods grow to nearly a metre and a half long. The seeds are a glossy dark brown and up to 6 cm across. Their outer coat is extremely tough. These beans are often washed out to sea and carried huge distances on ocean currents. They can survive in sea water for a year or more. In this way, they have established themselves on tropical shores throughout the world, exactly as the coconut has done. In the days when people used wax matches, bushmen hollowed out the seeds and used them as matchboxes.

Matchbox Bean

White-breasted Sea-eagles on their nest (photo: Belinda Wright)

119

PIED IMPERIAL-PIGEONS

Pied Imperial-Pigeons fly to their nesting island.

Pied Imperial-Pigeons, also called Nutmeg or Torres Strait Pigeons, migrate to Papua New Guinea in March and April, and return to the wet tropics in early August. They live in the lowlands, where they feed on rainforest fruit. One they favour is the native nutmeg. Soon after their return, thousands of the white birds may gather in a grove of fruiting trees to feed and to court. The males, puffing themselves out, boom their call "roo-ca-hooo". Their combined voices make the forests throb with sound.

While the birds may court on the mainland, they nest on offshore islands along the entire wet tropics coast. In that sense, they are birds of the rainforest edge. On some islands the pigeons nest in colonies numbering tens of thousands. Every evening, in flocks of just a few or several hundred, the birds fly to their nesting places. Once there, the pigeon relieves its partner which may have been incubating the single egg or looking after the nestling. The relieved parent flies to the mainland the next morning to spend the day feeding.

Hope Island, where the pigeons nest, is in the foreground. The birds feed in the rainforest of Cedar Bay National Park seen in the distance.

« Pied Imperial-Pigeons

Pied Imperial-Pigeon

The main advantage of nesting on the islands is the greatly reduced number of nest-robbing predators there. Black Butcherbirds, catbirds, goannas, rats and snakes are few or absent on the islands. The main disadvantage is that the birds must expend a great deal of energy flying to and fro, often against the strong tradewinds. They must also run the gauntlet of the White-breasted Sea-Eagles which share most of the islands with the pigeons.

The flocks of countless thousands of these beautiful black and white pigeons were once one of the great sights of the wet tropics. In the 1960s the birds were hunted almost to extinction. However, in recent years they have been better protected and have made a strong recovery.

A pigeon's nest

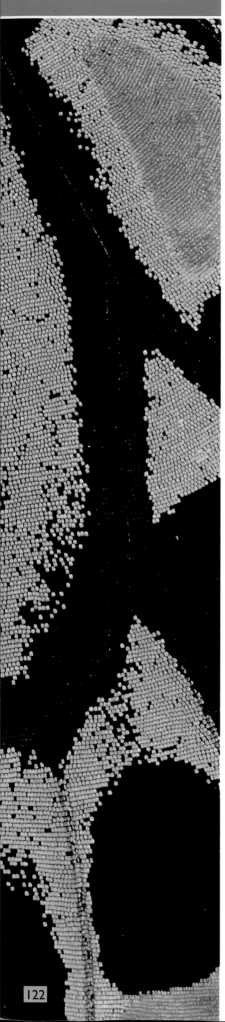

BUTTERFLIES

The rainforest edge, draped in vines (photo: Steve Parish)

Male Cairns Birdwing

Butterflies are everywhere in the wet tropics, but they are more easily seen along its rainforest edges, especially in the lowlands. Being mainly insects of the canopy, they come down to the lower strata here, where the canopy tilts down to ground level. Many species, including the Cairns Birdwing, the Red Lacewing and the cruiser, have caterpillars that feed on vines which are more prolific on the rainforest edge. It is possible to observe the life histories of many species — from the hatching of the egg to the mature butterfly emerging from its pupa.

Red Lacewing

If left unchecked, the caterpillars of butter-flies and moths would become so numerous that they would eat up the entire forest. But predators and parasites, from bugs to wasps and birds, keep caterpillar numbers in balance with their food supply.

However, the caterpillars have their defences. For example, swallowtail caterpillars, when attacked, swing their heads back and, from the back of the head, extrude a V-shaped, evil-smelling, red-coloured appendage called an osmeterium that discourages most predators. Other caterpillars absorb the poison of the plants they eat and so become poisonous themselves and immune from attack. Others again bribe such fierce predators as the weaver-ants with secretions of a sweet substance that the ants find irresistible. The ants become so fond of this food that they protect the caterpillars from the attacks of other insects. It is a fine balance, without excesses, in which both plants and animals live without annihilating each other.

An Assassin Bug eats the caterpillar of a Ulysses Butterfly.

Male Cruiser

« Close-up of the wing of a male Cairns Birdwing

Female Cruiser

Life history of the Green Spotted Triangle from caterpillar to pupa (top, from left) to fully developed butterfly (above right)

A caterpillar of an Orchard Butterfly defends itself.

Above, left to right: Weaver Ants catch and devour insects much larger than themselves, but they protect the caterpillars of the Oak Blue and related butterflies.

THE WORLD'S LARGEST MOTH

The Hercules Moth is the largest moth in the world, with a wingspan of 25 cm. It is so large that when you see one slowly flapping through the forest at dusk, you might mistake it for a bat. The moth lives from the lowlands to quite high altitudes. Usually it flies around the canopy, like the butterflies, so it is more easily observed along the forest edge.

Two kinds of food plants favoured by the moth's caterpillars are the Bleeding Heart and the Celery Wood trees. Both are pioneer species, and therefore are more common along the forest boundary.

Because this moth is so large, it is rewarding to examine its details in close-up — from its egg-laying, pupa, caterpillar and adult stages, to the scales on its wings and the male's feather-like antennae. In smaller moths these features would be discernible only under a microscope.

FIRE AND RAIN

Rose Gums and Alexandra Palms intermingle where rainforest and eucalypt forest meet.

On three sides, in the south, west and north, the wet tropics grade into dry forests composed mostly of such non-rainforest trees as eucalypts, wattles, turpentines and casuarinas. In the north, the rainforest border is in the lowlands, but everywhere else it is on one of the tablelands or on hill ranges. Where the two forests meet is an area of struggle for supremacy. The rainforest's main ally is, of course, frequent rainfall, while the eucalypt forests advance with the connivance of fire. During successive years of good rainfall, free of fire, the rainforest begins to colonise the domain of the eucalypts. Some of this territory is taken by stealth as strangler figs enmesh turpentine, paperbark or eucalypt trees, and vines snake up into their canopy. Epiphytes may establish themselves on the larger limbs.

Bottlebrush Orchid

Blossom Bat on eucalypt flowers

Red-sided Skink

The Lace Goanna is at home in both kinds of forest.

« *Top to bottom:* Flowers and fruit from the rainforest edge: Clerodendrum fruit; Hoya flowers; fruit of Lemon-fruit Pittosporum

Yellow Penda trees on the edge of the rainforest

Female Yellow-bellied Sunbird at its nest

Yellow Penda tree in full flower

A Rose Gum left isolated in the advancing rainforest

Yellow Penda among granite boulders

Metallic Starlings

A Crimson Finch feeds on grass seeds.

At ground level, the more vigorous rainforest trees, especially the pioneer species and vines, take up the space between mature dry forest trees. Their shade then stops the competition from regenerating. If no fire intervenes for several decades, the old-growth eucalypts and their allies grow in a rainforest understorey. Once the rainforest is firmly established, it tends to exclude fire and, after one or two hundred years, the eucalypts and turpentines will have died out, ceding their territory to the rainforest.

When rain is less reliable and fire more frequent, the rainforest retreats. Every fire claims a few more metres which do not regrow. Eucalypts, on the other hand, quickly regenerate after fire.

While it has been established that the present climatic era is encouraging rainforest to expand, frequent man-made fires actually cause them to shrink.

Yellow Penda

The narrow strip where this see-sawing battle takes place is full of fascinating plants and animals — massive flowering penda trees, delicate nectar-feeding bats, special orchids, vines and fruits. Certain reptiles and birds thrive in this zone.

Amethyst Python (photo Belinda Wright)

SAVING THE RAINFORESTS

"We are the generation for whom the only message for a tropical biologist is: Set aside your random research and devote your life to activities that will bring the world to understand that tropical nature is an integral part of human life. If our generation does not do it, it won't be there for the next."

D.H. JANZEN 1986

The rising sun, diffused by a faint haze, wraps the forest canopy in an opalescent light. A tree-kangaroo climbs to the topmost branches of an emergent tree to sunbathe, for most mornings are cool on the Atherton Tableland. The songs and calls of chowchillas, whipbirds, catbirds and others rise up from the forest floor 25 m below, where it is still twilight. Insectivorous bats and brushtail possums retire to tree hollows to sleep the day away. Scrubfowl scratch among the leaf-litter between boulders in their search for earthworms, beetles and other small ground life.

Suddenly, along the edge of the forest, an engine starts, a loud, angry sound that silences the birds. Red-legged Pademelons bound deeper into the undergrowth. After a few minutes warming up, the bulldozer's driver aims his machine at the nearest trees and begins his assault on the forest. Smaller trees and shrubs are up-rooted and pushed aside. Older, more robust trees offer greater resistance. Among these are Black Bean and tulip oak trees a hundred or more years old. Large or small, all are felled and reduced to heaps of detritus. The bulldozer's shining steel tracks crush festoons of delicate orchid flowers and epiphytic ferns knocked out of the canopy. Rare species, lacewoods, solo trees and others all meet the same indiscriminate fate.

The rumble of the heavy machine and the constant falling of trees shake the ground. A Yellow-footed Antechinus, a small insect-eating marsupial, dashes from its refuge in a hollow log splintered by the bulldozer, and dives into a narrow space between boulders. The machine compacts the rocks and crushes the marsupial. The nests of Purple-crowned Pigeons, Spectacled Flycatchers, Grey-headed Robins and others are knocked down.

Pigeons, figbirds, cuckoo-shrikes and other fruit-eating birds fly out of the fig tree they were feeding on minutes before it is pushed over. The mound of leaf-litter scraped together by a pair of scrubfowl to incubate their eggs is pushed aside. The six or seven eggs are smashed but a newly-hatched chick just evades the machine's blade and flies off into the forest. A Green Possum manages to cling to a severed vine that swings out of the bulldozer's way. Small bats twitter in a tree hollow and wheel off just as their home is pushed down. In another hollow in the same tree, a Coppery Brushtail Possum could not make its escape and crashes to the ground, still in its hollow. It emerges, blinking in the unfamiliar bright light, dazed but not seriously injured. But its home and the forest where it lived have been demolished.

The ground vibrations have woken a large Amethyst Python and it slowly slithers from a cavern between large boulders. A tree is uprooted and crashes across its coils, breaking the snake's back and pinning it to the ground, where it will writhe for a day or more before it dies. Several tree-kangaroos leap from their trees and dash out of the bulldozer's way. Hundreds of other animals — insects, lizards, frogs, snakes, mammals and birds have lost their homes, their livelihood or their very lives.

The tree-kangaroos and possums do not leave their destroyed territories. Neighbouring forests have no free niches for them. Most will die from starvation or the attacks of dingos and half-feral dogs.

When the felled forest has dried, it will be burned. All its life will then be extinguished. Grass seeds will be sown in the ashes and will in time grow to feed a few cattle. The rainforest is gone, most likely forever.

This chiselling away at the rainforest continues in the wet tropics in the late 1990s.

The endangered Common Mist Frog

Lumholtz's Tree-kangaroo

Lemuroid Ringtail Possum

« The white phase of the Lemuroid Ringtail Possum became a symbol in the campaign to save the rainforests during the 1980s. (photo: Andrew Dennis)

The Pied Imperial-Pigeon was almost hunted into extinction during the 1960s

In the late 1960s and early 1970s, the future of Australia's tropical rainforests hung in the balance. There was a real possibility that they would disappear. The forests were then still thought of as an alien intrusion from Asia; they were somehow non-Australian and valued only as a source of timber. When the timber had been extracted, there was great pressure to clear them for sugarcane growing along the coast, and for dairying and agriculture on the tablelands. At that time, the rainforests were not widely appreciated for their own intrinsic qualities. Forty percent of the rainforests that had existed before European settlement had already been cleared, and there were increasing pressures to alienate much of the remainder.

The rainforest's inherent values began to be researched and understood in the 1960s. Through the pioneering work of Len Webb, Geoff Tracey and a few others, it emerged that these were unique forests and that they had an Australian origin. At the same time, it was discovered that very little remained. Certain types of rainforests, the most complex of all, and in fact the most diverse of all Australian habitats, were about to disappear. These most complex rainforests grew on the lowlands, in sheltered areas with fertile soils. After exhaustive searches, Webb and Tracey could only find eight hectares of this type at Clump Point near Mission Beach, and 1000 hectares at McNamee Creek near the South Johnstone River. That was all. The forest at Clump Point has been all but swallowed up by development. The McNamee Creek forest was declared a National Park, but only after it had been exhaustively logged. Several centuries will have to pass before anyone can see Australia's most complex habitat in a climax, undisturbed state again.

Areas of a similar type, though not quite as complex, survive at Downey Creek, also near the South Johnstone River and in the Daintree–Cape Tribulation area. Other kinds of rainforests, such as palm swamps and upland rainforests on deep basalt soils, were also threatened.

At the same time people were illegally stripping whole forests of their orchids and epiphytic ferns, to be sold in nurseries and supermarkets. Clearing continued, especially on the lowlands. Vast forests between Cardwell and Tully were converted to grazing land by King Ranch, in the process dispossessing the Djirbal and Girramay Aboriginal people. Around Daintree, land was also being cleared for cattle grazing. Neither venture, in the end, proved viable, but the forests have gone.

Fears were held for some animal species. On the tablelands, the habitat of the unique rainforest possums was shrinking alarmingly. On the lowlands, the fragmentation of the rainforest, increasing traffic, and feral and domestic dogs took greater and greater toll on the cassowary, and its population declined alarmingly. On the off-shore islands from Cardwell to Cooktown, Pied Imperial-Pigeons were being shot in such numbers that if it continued the birds would soon be extinct. In a single shoot on North Brook Island, 1100 of the pigeons were killed during the 1967-68 nesting season. During the next season fewer than 2000 birds nested on the island, about a third of the numbers that came four years before that. In the late 1960s there was no cause for optimism for the survival of the tropical rainforests.

But the 1960s was also a decade of enlightenment and an awakening to the necessity of conserving the natural environment. With the increase in knowledge about the

« Many species of frog have disappeared from mountain streams like these.

forests, their plants and animals and their origins, and an awareness of the imminent extinction of important tracts, a groundswell of public support gained momentum. Australia is forever indebted to the Wildlife Preservation Society of Queensland (WPSQ) which began, in the 1960s, the struggle that eventually led to the tropical rainforests being inscribed on the World Heritage List. In 1980 the Cairns and Far North Queensland Environment Centre was formed. Through the Centre's tireless work, all of Australia became aware of what was at stake, and Australia responded with overwhelming support. Even so, the entrenched opposition of the Queensland Government to conserving the rainforest meant that some early battles were lost.

In November 1983, conservationists set up a blockade against the bulldozers that were poised to push a road from Cape Tribulation to the mouth of the Bloomfield River — through pristine rainforest. The road, being bulldozed willy-nilly without regard to engineering standards, would be disastrous, destroying creeks and lowland forests, and threatening to smother coral reefs with silt from the run-off from the inevitable massive erosion. The blockade managed to delay the road construction until the onset of the wet season when work became impossible.

The bulldozers gathered in the Cape Tribulation rainforests again in August 1984. The conservationists literally dug themselves in, and held the road-building juggernaut at bay. But after two weeks, they were excavated by machinery and overpowered by superior numbers of police. The road was pushed through. At the same time, land developers bought up large tracts of rainforest north of the Daintree River and subdivided it into small plots.

On the very day that the second Cape Tribulation blockade commenced, timber-cutters and their bulldozers and trucks were about to move into the Downey Creek forests, the last, unlogged tract of the most complex rainforest in Australia. The Innisfail Branch of the WPSQ organised a vigil on the logging road into Downey Creek. But, in the dead of night, the timber getters moved in and logging began at a frantic pace. Through the constant vigilance of the WPSQ, the logging company was forced to abide by all the Forest Department's guidelines — no roads or tracks too close to water courses, minimal erosion, only trees over a certain size could be cut and so on. These guidelines had not always been adhered to in the past.

There were successes. Near Cardwell, the Pied Imperial-Pigeons, as a direct result of conservationists' campaigns, were better protected on their nesting islands. This protection bore spectacular results. By the 1985-6 nesting season, 22 000 pigeons came to North Brook Island. Once again the island throbbed with their calls. There were similar increases on other nesting islands. But the pigeons were still not entirely safe, for the future of the mainland forests, where they fed, was still uncertain.

By the early 1980s there was such a push for timber extraction that smaller and smaller trees were allowed to be cut. It became obvious that if these pressures continued, all the tropical rainforests not protected in national parks, which was still the largest area, would be severely damaged, if not totally destroyed. It was also clear that selective, sustainable logging of the forests would not support a vigorous logging industry in the long run.

But because of these forests' unique plant and animal life, they are beyond economic value — they hold several keys to our study and understanding of life on earth. In any case, the newly-burgeoning tourism industry was fast outstripping timber extraction in economic worth, and visitors came to experience living, complex, undisturbed forests. It was self-evident that the remaining tropical rainforests should be preserved and that the best way to do that was under World Heritage Listing.

The Queensland Government and the logging industry strenuously resisted the idea. Many of the people who were involved in the struggles of the 1970s and early 1980s came to the defence of the rainforests again. In January of 1984, the Rainforest Conservation Society of Queensland (RCSQ) undertook to evaluate and report on the criteria that are to be met for inclusion in the World Heritage List. In the process they consulted a wide range of researchers in many different fields, and gained support from the Federal Government.

The criteria for inclusion on the World Heritage List are strict. The area proposed must meet at least one of the following criteria:

1. be an outstanding example representing the major stages of the earth's evolutionary history;
2. be an outstanding example representing significant on-going geological and ecological processes, biological evolution and humanity's interaction with the natural environment;
3. contain superlative natural phenomena, formations or features;
4. contain the most important and significant natural habitats where threatened species of animals and plants of outstanding universal value...still survive.

Such is the value of Australia's tropical rainforests that they fulfil not just one criterion, but all four. Few places in the world do.

In December 1988, 9000 sq km of north Queensland's wet tropics were inscribed on the World Heritage List. Of this, 6300 sq km are tropical rainforest, which is 83 per cent of all the rainforest that remained. The other 17 per cent is mostly in private hands. All logging was banned in the listed area and large-scale clearing was no longer possible. For the time being at least, the forests were saved.

In the 1990s, therefore, the future of the forests, and their plants and animals, seems assured. The Pied Imperial-Pigeons continue to thrive. Tree kangaroos and rainforest possums and their habitats are secure.

The Waterfall Torrent Frog has disappeared from the higher altitudes.

Some environmental repairs have begun. The Wet Tropics Management Authority is spending millions of dollars in buying back rainforest land, improving roads, and rehabilitating cleared land north of the Daintree River. Feral pigs, which can devastate the forest understorey, are being eradicated. This "Daintree Rescue" became necessary to maintain the integrity of these unique forests.

The Sharp-snouted Day Frog is near extinction.

Yet all is not well, even now. The threats are more insidious. The most baffling problem is that of the disappearing stream-living frogs, which is a world-wide phenomenon. In Australia's wet tropics, thirteen species of frogs live most or all of their lives around fast-flowing streams and waterfalls. Four of these, the Armoured Mist Frog, the Mountain Mist Frog, the Sharp-snouted Day Frog and the Northern Tinker Frog have not been seen for years. These are presumed to be extinct. Others such as the Waterfall Frog, Common Mist Frog and Lace-lid Frog have disappeared from the uplands and highlands, where they were once common, but

The Northern Tinker Frog has not been seen for years

remain in the lowlands. Another species, the Green-eyed Tree Frog, declined drastically, but is making a comeback. The cause of the extinctions and decline is still unknown despite much research. The puzzling thing is that the places in the higher altitudes, where the depletion is the greatest, are the least disturbed and freest of pollution. Reduction of the ozone layer and global warming have been ruled out as causes for the decline. Most of the disappearing frogs finally die of some disease, but only after they have been weakened by another as yet unknown cause.

Flying foxes are also dying in unprecedented numbers. In their case a major cause is known — attack by paralysis-inducing ticks.

The threats to the cassowary continue. Dogs and traffic still kill the birds in significant numbers. On the lowlands between Innisfail and Tully, where possibly the largest number of these birds live, their habitat continues to be fragmented as privately-owned forests are cleared. Vital corridors that link feeding areas are being destroyed. The last known wild cassowary in the city of Cairns was killed by two dogs in 1996.

Important forests still in private hands are being cleared on the Atherton Tableland. Part of a forest near Yungaburra, which contains the densest known population of Lumholtz's Tree-kangaroos, was cleared in 1996. Several tree kangaroos died as a result.

At Oyster Point, near Cardwell, close to pristine Hinchinbrook Island National Park, state and federal governments have given approval for the development of a resort that scientists

The introduction of the Cane Toad has led to the decline of many native species of animal.

« This Lumholtz's Tree-kangaroo did not survive the destruction of its habitat. (photo: Graeme Newell)

The Lace-lid Frog has disappeared from the highlands but survives in the lowlands.

northern Queensland's tropical rainforests, uniquely Australian forests that have grown here ever since tropical rainforest existed on this planet, will be preserved for everyone to experience.

Rainforest cleared and burnt (photo: Graeme Newell)

believe will have a detrimental effect on the criteria set down for World Heritage Listing — values that the governments are bound to defend. At the same time, millions are being spent on the Daintree rescue to correct similar mistakes made in the past.

A change in attitude emerged in the mid-1990s, especially in government circles: that these forests must be harnessed for economic gain. Consequently, the opportunity to experience them, to move about in them, to be stimulated by them, and to be intellectually challenged by them, has become a potential "product" to be sold. Once again the forests have become a mere resource, a provider of raw materials, that must be exploited. We have come full circle.

A report, published by the CSIRO in 1996, states that many areas of the wet tropics rainforest are degraded, that some unique types of forest are not protected and that weeds, feral animals and fire management are still posing serious problems. We must remain vigilant so that

Flying foxes appear to be in decline in the wet tropics.

Satin Bowerbird

PART FIVE

ENJOYING THE RAINFORESTS

"In the process of getting acquainted [with tropical rainforest], this relationship develops according to the interest, capacity, keenness, curiosity and fantasy of the person, and to such a relationship there is no end."

MARIUS JACOBS IN 'THE TROPICAL RAINFOREST: A FIRST ENCOUNTER', 1988.

Australia's tropical rainforests comprise one of the world's great natural regions. They offer the visitor an almost unlimited variety of experiences, from the quiet contemplation of the plants and insects to the physical challenge of hiking in the wilderness and from swimming with turtles and platypuses in a cold mountain pool to the rush of white-water rafting. Whether to the beaches, the tablelands or the mountains, your visit will be stimulating, exciting and enjoyable. You will be steeped in the region's grandeur and feel the pull of its mystery.

The following pages are intended to help you plan your excursions into these rainforests, so you can experience the delights they offer without danger or undue discomfort.

Swimming and diving at Millaa Millaa Falls on the Atherton Tableland

« This immense White Fig tree on the edge of Lake Barrine is one of the countless wonders to be explored in Queensland's tropical rainforests.

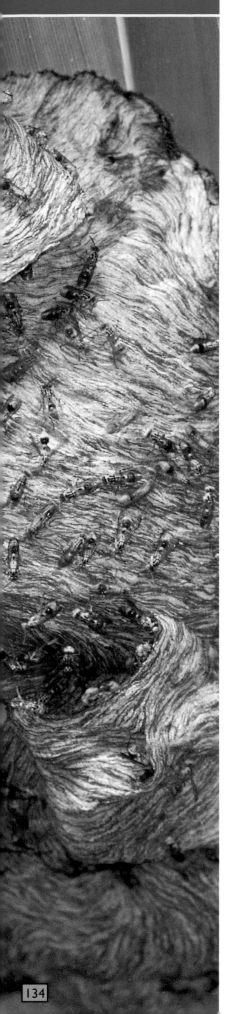

WHEN TO VISIT

Except when the roads are cut by wet season floods, which does not happen every year, most places can be visited at any time. Each season has its own attractions, both in terms of what you may see in the way of plants and animals and in climate.

The so-called winter months, from June to early September, are the coolest and can be dry. However, heavy and persistent rain, as well as prolonged drizzle, can occur during any month. In "winter" there are times of glorious warm days in the lowlands and bracing cool ones on the tablelands. Mosquitoes, leeches and some other irritants are then fewest, although they are seldom absent altogether. While the temperatures remain pleasant on the tablelands all the year round, the lowlands begin to warm up in September. November and the following few months are hot. September, October and November are the driest months. By December, thunderstorms are increasingly common and the season's first cyclone may threaten the coast.

September through January is the breeding season for many species of birds. Bowerbirds sing and display. Such migrants as the Pied Imperial-Pigeons, Metallic Starlings and White-tailed Kingfishers return from their wintering grounds in Papua New Guinea and begin to nest. On the tablelands, especially, the forests resound with prolonged concerts of bird song — more than at any other time of year.

The monsoon usually arrives some time in late December or January and lasts until the end of March or early April. Heavy rain, alternating with hot sunshine, creates an explosion of plant growth and insect activity. While mosquitoes are common, this is also the time when you see most butterflies and beetles. Fruits of trees, shrubs and vines are at their most varied and plentiful. Pigeons and catbirds, cassowaries and figbirds, Musky Rat-kangaroos and flying-foxes can eat their fill as in no other season. Fungi proliferate in an infinity of shapes and colours.

In April all this activity, as well as the heavy monsoon rain, tapers off. The next few months can be balmy sunshine or drizzling rain, especially on the eastern tablelands and the Daintree–Cape Tribulation areas. But wet forests are vibrant forests. Dab on some insect repellent to keep the leeches away, and enter the forest to feel this vibrancy and to be exhilarated by rain in the rainforest.

PHOTOGRAPHY

The grandeur, mystery and romance of the great tropical forests, and the exotic plants and animals that inhabit them, are the stuff of nature photographers' dreams. Yet, apart from the wide vistas from open vantage points, photography in the rainforest can be disappointing. The sun dappling on the forest floor on a bright day, so pleasing to the eye, comes out in a patchwork of black and pale green, with little or no detail, in most photographs. On an overcast day, when there are no sun flecks, the light is so low that it barely registers on your camera's light meter. The light on overcast days also has a bluish tinge, which on some kinds of film makes the forest look less green than it should be. Trees and vines crowd so closely together that it is difficult to get the forest's perspective, or to go back far enough from a large buttressed tree, for example, to see it all in your viewfinder.

Tree buttresses and other plants in the rainforest are best photographed during bright but overcast weather.

There are a few simple techniques and aides that will solve most of these problems:
• Nothing can be done about wide-angle photographs in a sun-dappled forest. Film, unlike the human eye, cannot register detail in both shady and sunny patches: the difference in light intensity is just too great. You must expose either for the dark areas or for the sunlit ones. Photographs of a subject, such as a backlit leaf or spider web, in a single sun fleck can be most effective, however.
• Flash can be used to great advantage for plants and animals and details of trees or rocks. It is ineffective in wide shots of the forest.
• Wide-angle photographs of a single large tree or a whole forest work wonderfully well during an overcast day — especially if the cloud cover is light when there are no extremes of contrast between sun and shade. But these kinds of photographs cannot be taken with a hand-held camera, as the exposures are too long. If there is no convenient branch or rock where you can rest your camera, you must use a sturdy tripod and a cable release. The cable release is necessary so

« Paperwasps on their nest

that you do not bump the camera as you press the shutter-release button. Even the slightest vibration will blur your picture. Do not be afraid of exposures of a minute or more.

• The light on overcast days has a blue tinge. On some films this gives the foliage a strange, cold, blue-green look. To a degree, this can be compensated for by using a light amber filter.

• Because the trees grow so closely together, you cannot always move back far enough to get your entire subject in the frame. The use of an extra-wide-angle lens, such as 21 mm to 24 mm for 35 mm cameras, in most cases will let you get everything you want in a single picture. Unfortunately these kinds of lenses flatten out the perspective. They make huge and ancient trees look like saplings and towering rock formations like heaps of pebbles. If you are a serious photographer, with deep pockets, you can solve this problem by using a medium or large format camera. Their extra-wide-angle lenses do not distort the perspective nearly as much.

HAZARDS AND IRRITATIONS

Compared to those of other continents, Australia's tropical rainforests are benevolent to the human visitor. Nonetheless, it should be remembered that many of the forests of the wet tropics are true wilderness areas, not sanitised, made-safe theme parks, and there are several potential hazards and irritations that could spoil your visit. However, there is little to threaten you if you use common sense and observe a few simple precautions. It depends entirely on you how safe you are. If you approach the rainforests as truly wild places, they offer exciting experiences to everyone. Just keep a wary eye on the following:

• One of the rainforest's most common dangers is not some biting or stinging animal, but slippery rocks. The constant moisture, especially around waterfalls and swift-flowing streams, causes the growth of slime-like moulds, mosses and lichens. These can be very slippery, so rock-hop with care.

• Despite its name, the Saltwater Crocodile cruises well beyond the tidal zone of rivers and creeks. It also favours freshwater swamps close to the beach. But as long as you do not wade or swim in streams or lagoons likely to be inhabited by crocodiles, you will be safe from these giant reptiles.

Death Adder. Dangerous snakes are rarely seen in the rainforest

Marchfly

• The bullrout or freshwater stonefish, a fish that lives in the freshwater reaches of lowland streams, can give you a nasty sting if you step on it. Its habit is to lie motionless among rocks or weeds in backwaters and other areas away from the strongest currents. The 20 to 30 cm fish relies on its resemblance to the rocks, in its colour and shape, to remain undetected by such prey as shrimps and small fish which are snapped up when they come within range. Unlike other fish, bullrout do not, as a rule, get out of your way. When you step on one, the fish raises its dorsal fin, which has needle-sharp poisonous spines. The spines are so sharp that they will go through soft-soled shoes. The stings inflicted are very painful, but the pain can be alleviated by bathing the affected area in hot water.

• When you visit those magical places where the rainforest meets the beach, especially in summer, the temptation is to rush into the sea to swim. Do not be tempted. The Box Jellyfish inhabits the coastal shallows between November and May and it is dangerous. The clear-bodied jellyfish are virtually invisible in the water. They trail long tentacles

Tiger Leech

covered with stinging cells. When these cells come into contact with your skin, they cause intense pain and their effect can be fatal. If you do get stung, the most effective first aid is to pour copious amounts of vinegar over the stings. This neutralises the venom. Do not rub the area. You should get to a hospital as quickly as possible so that antivenine can be administered.

• The most commonly seen snakes in the rainforest are pythons and tree snakes. They are harmless. You may also see small to tiny species, some of which are venomous, but they are too small to worry you. There are a few potentially dangerous snakes in the rainforest such as the Red-bellied Black Snake and the Death Adder. The Taipan, whose bite can be fatal, does not live inside the rainforest, but in grassy areas outside it or along its edge. These dangerous species are rarely seen and try to get quickly out of your way, nearly always before you've even seen them. Unless you provoke them by catching them, or pushing and prodding them with sticks, there is no reason to fear these snakes. Watch where you walk, and if you are concerned about being bitten, wear boots, thick socks and long trousers.

• Cassowaries nearly always move away when they encounter people, although there are a few inquisitive ones in popularly visited places which may come and have a close look at you. They are not habitually aggressive towards humans. Only when defending their young or being suddenly confronted will they threaten by making a booming sound or attempting a kick. If you have the good fortune to meet a cassowary, move slowly away and dodge behind the trunks of trees. Do not turn your back and run.

• The animals mentioned so far that can make life difficult are large, easily seen and easily avoided. There are others which are more insidious. Some of these biting or stinging animals are so small you can barely see them with the naked eye. Others move so gently that they have bitten you and sucked some of your blood before you are even aware of it. But these annoying animals can also be avoided.

Of these smaller animals, leeches are probably the most often encountered. They are also the least harmful; they simply relieve you of a little blood. Leeches are worms which have evolved from earthworms. They are equipped with a sucker at both the mouth and tail ends. The sucker at the tail end is the larger. It is used for crawling about, but it also firmly attaches the animal to its host. Rainforest leeches, of which there are several species, appear when the ground and foliage are damp — which is quite often. They lie in wait for "prey", mostly warm-blooded animals, in the leaf-litter, on logs, and on the leaves of low bushes. They have several kinds of sensors along their body that enable them to detect movement, scents and changes in temperature. They are unerringly attracted to movement and warm bodies.

When it attaches to a victim, the leech moves about until it finds a place where it can penetrate the skin. The leech then cuts through the skin with its three semi-circular, toothed jaws. Once a blood supply has been tapped into, the leech secretes saliva from ducts located close to its jaws. The saliva contains a lubricating mucus, a mild anaesthetic (so you do not feel the bite), and an anti-coagulant that stops the blood from clotting, which would stop the flow. If left undisturbed, the leech is satiated in about half an hour, by which time it is hugely distended. It can take in seven to nine times its own empty body weight. Once full, the leech drops off and crawls awkwardly into some crevice or into the soil. Its meal will last it for more than a month; in some cold-climate species it lasts for a year. During a prolonged dry spell, leeches will worm their way into the soil and become dry and shrunken. They can survive in that state for months if necessary.

When a leech drops from its host, the cut it made in the skin continues to bleed for some

Fruit of the Lacewing Vine

time as a result of the injected anti-coagulant. Often the first signs of a leech bite is that some of your clothing is blood-soaked — usually your socks. However, the bites are clean and you will not catch anything from them, but they may itch for some days.

Insect repellent, especially when applied to your boots, socks and the skin above your socks, will keep you virtually leech free.

• Not so innocent, and accompanied by far more severe itching, is the bite of the larva of a small mite known appropriately as scrub itch. These larvae live in rotting logs and piles of leaf-litter on the forest floor. If you sit on a log, or crawl about in the litter, to photograph a fungus perhaps, the mite larvae will move up your limbs until they reach some restrictions in your clothing — usually your upper legs and waist. Here the larvae burrow in and suck your blood. The first you realise that you have "scrub itch" is an intolerable itchiness and large red welts. The larvae are so small, the size of a pinhead or less, that you may not even see them. You can get rid of them by applying alcohol (methylated spirits) or insect repellent to the bites. But by that time the damage has been done. You will itch severely for some days. Worse still, the mites carry scrub typhus, a rickettsial, debilitating disease. Fortunately it is quite rare. Again, you can keep scrub itch at bay with insect repellent.

• Fortunately, the scrub tick, Ixodes holocyclus, is rarer than the scrub itch mite. It is mostly found in upland forests. It is also larger, growing to about the size of a match head. When this tick pierces your skin to suck your blood, it injects a small amount of poison at the same time. As a result, the bite swells and you may suffer headaches. The tick should not be pulled out alive, but killed with alcohol or insect repellent before you remove it.

• Worldwide, and especially in the tropics, the animals that cause the most illness and kill the largest number of humans are the mosquitoes. They carry several diseases, the most serious of which is malaria. Fortunately, there is no malaria in Australia. The diseases mosquitoes do carry here, while debilitating for long periods, are rarely fatal. The two most serious are dengue fever and Ross River fever. Mosquitoes are far more numerous on the lowlands than on the uplands. Tropical strength insect repellent will protect you.

• Plants also carry poisons. Therefore it is best not to eat any rainforest fruit or fungi. Also, the sap of some trees is a severe skin irritant. With due care you can avoid these potential hazards, but one plant can inflict serious, long-lasting pain if you just brush against you.

It pays to learn to identify the stinging tree, or Gympie Stinger. The shrub's heart-shaped, large

« Fruit of the River Cherry or Bamaga Satinash floating in a pool

Noah Creek in Daintree National Park

leaves are covered with fine, stiff hairs — minuscule needles tipped with poison. When you brush against the leaves or stems, these tiny needles stick into your skin and stay there, causing severe pain. During the first 24 hours the pain is at its worst. Lesser pain persists for months, arising every time the affected area becomes wet. There is no known antidote. Shaving or using hair-removing wax may remove some of the poisonous hairs, but it does not eliminate their effects completely.

• Because the rainforest's vegetation is so dense, it is sometimes difficult to see where you are going or where you have been, and it is easy to become lost. If you are tempted to go off the beaten track, make sure you let someone know and have a good compass and detailed maps with you.

Do not let the rainforest stingers and biters deter you. The tropical rainforest is not a fearsome or brutal place — quite the contrary. If you use common sense and do not go swimming with the Estuarine Crocodiles and Box Jellyfish, if you use insect repellent, and watch out for slippery rocks, you are as safe in the rainforest as in any other wild place.

THE RESERVES

To experience the rainforest fully, visit a variety of reserves, including national parks, state forests, environmental parks and other places administered by local shires and city councils. In quite a few parks, it is possible to camp for a nominal fee. A permit is needed to enter certain state forests. These can be readily obtained from the offices of the Department of Natural Resources.

For convenience the region has been divided into five sections.

For access to the reserves see the maps.

SECTION ONE: TOWNSVILLE TO CARDWELL

PALUMA RANGE NATIONAL PARK

 Department of Environment
PMB 16
PALUMA QLD 4816

This National Park consists of three small areas on the Paluma and Seaview Ranges. The central part, on top of the Paluma Range, is the most accessible. At an altitude of more than 800 m, the rainforest here is of the mountain type. These are the southernmost of Australia's wet tropics rainforests and are less diverse than those of the wetter regions further north. As an introduction to the rainforests, however, they are superb. You can see many kinds of birds, such as the Grey-headed Robin and Golden Bowerbird, which are unique to the higher altitudes. The forests also give you a feel of how the drier habitats, dominated by eucalypts, casuarinas and banksias, were derived from rainforest and how the two kinds of forests grade into each other. There are sweeping views of the coast, the drier hills and granite rock formations.

Further north, at the base of the Seaview Range, is the Jourama Falls section of the park. Rainforest is confined to the deep gullies along streams.

BROADWATER STATE FOREST PARK

 Department of Natural Resources
PO Box 1650
INGHAM QLD 4850

This small Recreation Park in the Herbert River Valley is part of the Abergowrie State Forest. Only small portions are lowland-type rainforests. Along a 2-km walking track stands a gigantic, buttressed fig tree.

LUMHOLTZ NATIONAL PARK

This large, 124 000 hectare National Park runs from the sea at the Hinchinbrook Channel, across the Seaview, Gorge and Cardwell Ranges, almost to the source of the Herbert River. Only parts of the eastern slopes and the hilltops are covered with rainforest, which ranges from mangroves and lowland types to those of the uplands. The park is named after the Norwegian naturalist Carl Lumholtz, who explored the rainforests of this area in 1882. He was the first European to collect many of the unique rainforest animals, such as one of the two species of tree kangaroo and several possums.

Vehicle and walking access to this park are limited. Only the most intrepid and experienced bushwalkers should attempt to venture far into its forests. However, two places can be readily enjoyed.

Dalrymple Gap Walking Track

 Department of Environment
PO Box 1293
INGHAM QLD 4850

The 8-km walking track follows a section of a trail originally established by the area's Aborigines. Aboriginal tracks once criss-crossed the entire wet tropics. In 1864, the explorer and grazier George Dalrymple, after establishing Cardwell as a seaport, used this same trail as a stock route to the grazing lands beyond the ranges. Remnants of this route such as road cuttings, a stone bridge and other works can still be seen. The track climbs through open eucalypt forest, with ribbons of rainforest along the gullies, to the Gap. The descent into Dalrymple Creek, however, is through rainforest. After several more creek crossings, the track reaches the carpark at Abergowrie State Forest, close to the Broadwater State Forest Park.

« Scaly Tree Ferns on the rainforest edge

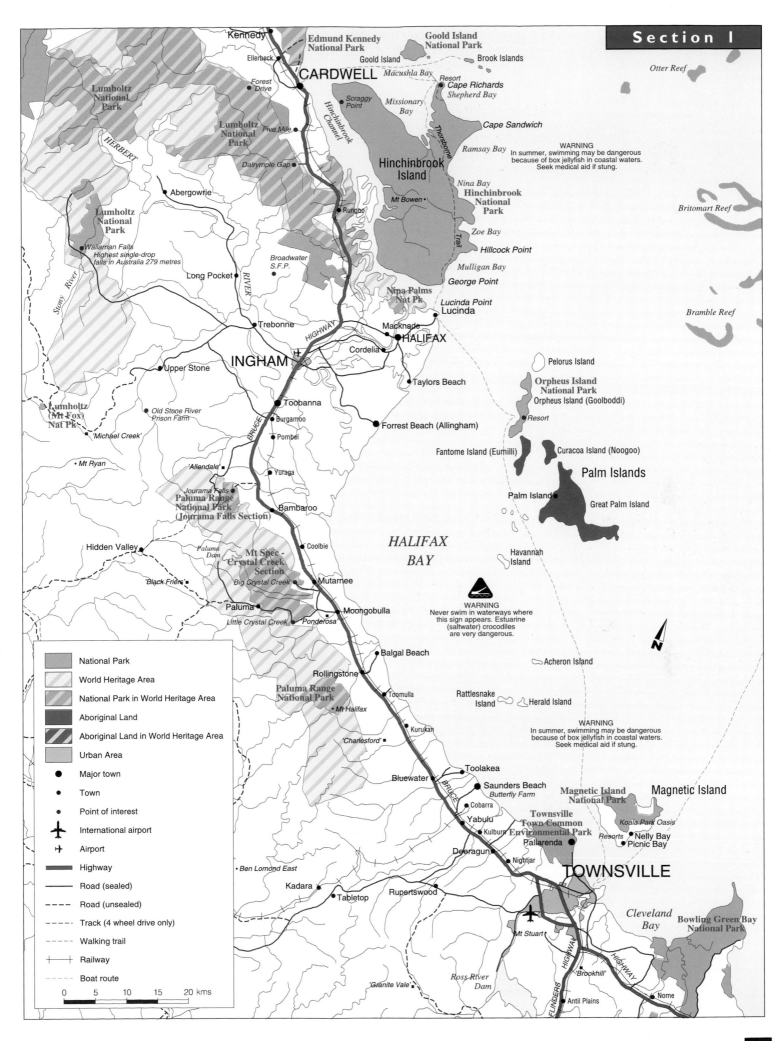

Kennedy

Ellerbeck

Edmund Kennedy National Park

Goold Island National Park

Goold Island

Brook Islands

CARDWELL

Macushla Bay

Resort

Cape Richards

Shepherd Bay

Otter Reef

Lumholtz National Park

Forest Drive

Scraggy Point

Missionary Bay

Cape Sandwich

HERBERT

Lumholtz National Park

Five Mile

Hinchinbrook Channel

Ramsay Bay

WARNING
In summer, swimming may be dangerous because of box jellyfish in coastal waters. Seek medical aid if stung.

Dalrymple Gap

Hinchinbrook Island

Britomart Reef

Abergowrie

Thorsborne Trail

Nina Bay

Hinchinbrook National Park

Rungoo

Mt Bowen

Lumholtz National Park

Wallaman Falls
Highest single-drop falls in Australia 279 metres

Stony River

Broadwater S.F.P.

Zoe Bay

Hillcock Point

Long Pocket

RIVER

Mulligan Bay

George Point

Bramble Reef

Nipa-Palms Nat Pk

Lucinda Point

Lucinda

Trebonne

HIGHWAY

Macknade

HALIFAX

Upper Stone

INGHAM

Cordelia

Taylors Beach

Pelorus Island

Lumholtz (Mt Fox) Nat Pk

Old Stone River Prison Farm

Toobanna

Orpheus Island National Park
Orpheus Island (Goolboddi)

BRUCE

Burgamoo

Resort

'Michael Creek'

Pombel

Forrest Beach (Allingham)

Fantome Island (Eumilli)

Curacoa Island (Noogoo)

Mt Ryan

'Allendale'

Yuraga

Palm Islands

Paluma Range National Park (Jourama Falls Section)

Jourama Falls

Bambaroo

Palm Island

Great Palm Island

Hidden Valley

Paluma Dam

Coolbie

Mt Spec - Crystal Creek Section

HALIFAX BAY

Havannah Island

'Black Friers'

Big. Crystal Creek

Mutarnee

Paluma

Moongobulla

'Ponderosa'

Little Crystal Creek

WARNING
Never swim in waterways where this sign appears. Estuarine (saltwater) crocodiles are very dangerous.

Balgal Beach

Acheron Island

Rollingstone

Paluma Range National Park

Toomulla

Rattlesnake Island

Herald Island

Mt Halifax

Kurukan

'Charlesford'

WARNING
In summer, swimming may be dangerous because of box jellyfish in coastal waters. Seek medical aid if stung.

N

Toolakea

Bluewater

BRUCE

Saunders Beach
Butterfly Farm

Magnetic Island National Park

Magnetic Island

Cobarra

Yabulu

Koala Park Oasis

Kulburn

Townsville Town Common Environmental Park

Resorts

Nelly Bay

Pallarenda

Picnic Bay

Deeragun

Nightjar

Ben Lomond East

TOWNSVILLE

Kadara

Tabletop

Rupertswood

Cleveland Bay

Bowling Green Bay National Park

Mt Stuart

'Brookhill'

'Granite Vale'

Ross River Dam

FLINDERS

HIGHWAY

HIGHWAY

Antill Plains

Nome

Legend

	National Park
	World Heritage Area
	National Park in World Heritage Area
	Aboriginal Land
	Aboriginal Land in World Heritage Area
	Urban Area
●	Major town
•	Town
•	Point of interest
✈	International airport
✈	Airport
	Highway
	Road (sealed)
	Road (unsealed)
	Track (4 wheel drive only)
	Walking trail
	Railway
	Boat route

0 5 10 15 20 kms

Wallaman Falls

Department of Environment
PO Box 1293
INGHAM   QLD 4850

The waters of Stony Creek, a substantial perennial stream, plunge over a sheer cliff at Wallaman Falls. The fall is 279 m, the highest single-drop falls in Australia and one of the most spectacular. There are great views across the gorge at the top lookout, which is surrounded by open eucalypt forest. When the water thunders down after heavy rain, the narrow gorge is filled with spray and mist. This moisture ensures the growth of rainforest. The pool at the bottom of Wallaman Falls is 20 m deep.

A 2-km walking track winds down through this forest into the gorge. It is an exhilarating walk with ever-closer views of the falls. Should you wish to walk beyond the base of the falls you need to obtain a permit from the Department of Environment office in Ingham.

HINCHINBROOK ISLAND NATIONAL PARK

Department of Environment
Box 74
CARDWELL QLD 4849

At 39 350 hectares, Hinchinbrook Island is Australia's largest island national park ,and one of the wet tropics' three truly outstanding reserves. Apart from a small non-intrusive resort at Cape Richards, there are no human settlements, roads or other developments. Little evidence remains of earlier attempts at settlement, which were abandoned in the early 1930s. The forests were logged, however. Numerous shell middens and the remains of a stone fish trap at Scraggy Point are indications of Aboriginal people's long association with the island.

Hinchinbrook is one of the few places where you can have a true wilderness experience in the wet tropics. A mosaic of eucalypt and paperbark woodlands, heaths and rainforests rise from extensive mangrove forests to high, rugged granite peaks. Near the centre of the island, Mount Bowen is the highest at 1121 m. You need to be a fit and experienced bushwalker to climb this mountain. A permit from the Department of Environment is required.

The mangroves are most satisfyingly explored in a small boat. For a closer look there are boardwalks at Ramsay Bay. The broadleafed lowland rainforests are most easily seen in protected gullies along the east coast. But these forests are drier than those further north and, as a consequence, are less complex. A series of walking tracks between Macushla and Shepherd Bay give a taste of this kind of forest. But to fully savour them you should walk the 32 km long Thorsborne Trail, one of the country's great bushwalks. The trail is named for the late Arthur Thorsborne in recognition of his untiring efforts in environmental conservation in the wet tropics, especially for his beloved Hinchinbrook. The trail, while marked, is ungraded and walkers need to be self-sufficient. The four- to five-day walk includes beaches, creeks, waterfalls, mangrove forests, palm swamps and rainforests, as well as the drier heaths and woodlands.

This scene at Bramston Beach is typical of many coastal reserves.

« Flame Tree

Wallaman Falls

SECTION TWO: CARDWELL TO INNISFAIL

EDMUND KENNEDY NATIONAL PARK

 Department of Environment
Box 74
CARDWELL QLD 4849

This 6200 hectare park is mostly wetlands which back on to the beaches of Rockingham Bay. It was here that Edmund Kennedy came ashore in 1848 to begin his ill-fated exploration of Cape York Peninsula. His expedition spent more than a month at Rockingham Bay cutting its way through the forests and swamps.

Rainforest occurs only along the beach and freshwater streams. A series of boardwalks and walking tracks at the southern end of the park give you the opportunity to experience the forests without the difficulties and frustrations Kennedy encountered. The place has changed little, if at all, since his day.

Do not forget your insect repellent, as mosquitoes and midges (sand flies) can be numerous and persistent.

The camping ground at Murray Falls

MURRAY FALLS STATE FOREST PARK

 Department of Natural Resources
PO Box 312
CARDWELL QLD 4849

This small reserve, consisting of a mixture of lowland rainforest and eucalypt forest, centres around a series of falls, rapids and large pools on the Murray River. The water rushes over extensive formations of water-sculpted and polished granite rock. It is a most popular swimming spot. A short walking track through rainforest ascends to a lookout with views of waterfalls, hills and forests. Signboards along the track explain how Aboriginal people lived in these forests.

TULLY GORGE STATE FOREST PARK

 Department of Natural Resources
PO Box 312
CARDWELL QLD 4849

The Tully Gorge is one of the wettest regions of Australia and the lowland forests are lush and complex. However, they were thoroughly logged in the recent past, so there are few accessible large trees. The Tully River, a popular river for white-water rafting and kayaking, races through impressive basalt rock formations. Walking through riverside forests, around rock pools and along reaches of wild water, is the chief pleasure for those who prefer to stay dry. The gorge is especially rich in butterflies, other insects and frogs.

The head of the valley is only a few kilometres from Tully Gorge National Park, at the southern end of the Atherton Tableland. There is no road or track connecting the two.

« Moss growing on a log

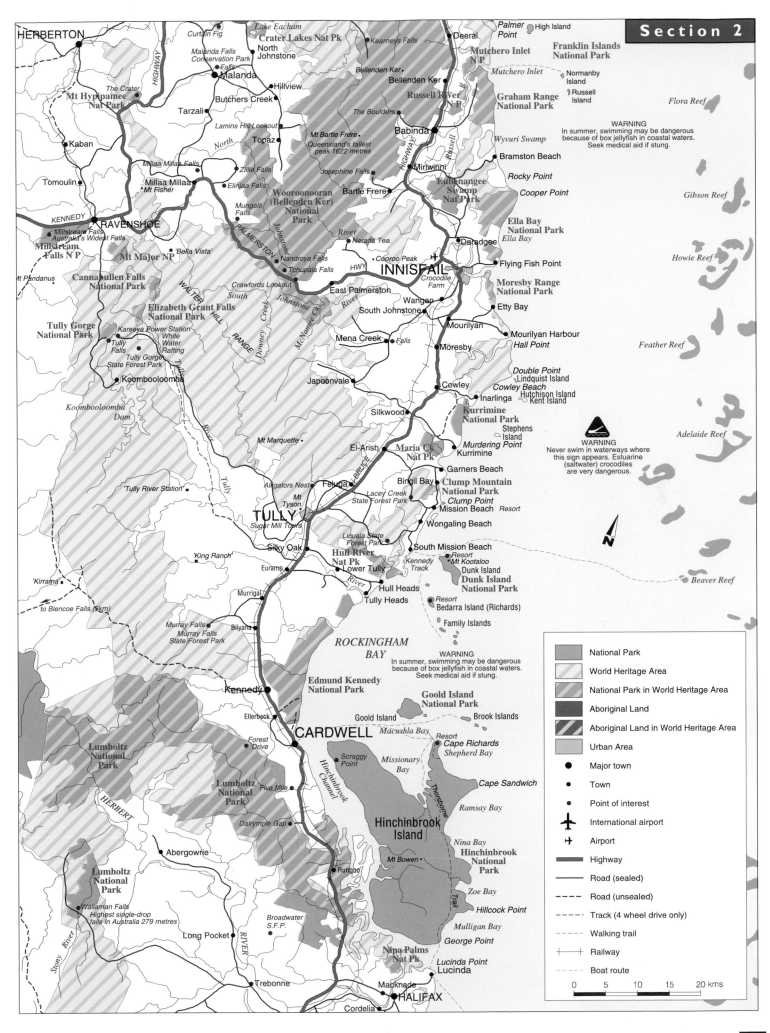

HERBERTON

Lake Eacham
Curtain Fig
Crater Lakes Nat Pk
North Johnstone
Kearneys Falls
Palmer Point • High Island
Deeral
Mutchero Inlet N P
Franklin Islands National Park

Malanda Falls Conservation Park
Malanda
Falls
The Crater
Mt Hypipamee Nat Park
Butchers Creek
Hillview
Bellenden Ker
Bellenden Ker
Russell River N P
Mutchero Inlet
Normanby Island
Russell Island
Flora Reef

Tarzali
Lamins Hill Lookout
The Boulders
Babinda
Graham Range National Park

Kaban
North
Topaz
Mt Bartle Frere •
Queensland's tallest peak 1622 metres
Miriwinni
Wyvuri Swamp

WARNING
In summer, swimming may be dangerous because of box jellyfish in coastal waters. Seek medical aid if stung.

Millaa Millaa Falls
Zillie Falls
Josephine Falls
Bramston Beach
Rocky Point

Tomoulin
Millaa Millaa
• Mt Fisher
Elinjaa Falls
Mungalli Falls
Bartle Frere
Eubenangee Swamp Nat Park
Cooper Point
Gibson Reef

KENNEDY
RAVENSHOE
Wooroonooran (Bellenden Ker) National Park
River
Nerada Tea
Ella Bay National Park
Ella Bay

Millstream Falls
Australia's Widest Falls
Millstream Falls N P
Mt Major NP
'Bella Vista'
Nandroya Falls
Tchupala Falls
• *Cooroo Peak*
Daradgee
INNISFAIL
Crocodile Farm
Flying Fish Point
Howie Reef

Mt Pandanus
Cannabullen Falls National Park
South
Crawfords Lookout
East Palmerston
Wangan
South Johnstone
Moresby Range National Park

Elizabeth Grant Falls National Park
WALTER HILL RANGE
PALMERSTON
Johnstone
HWY
River
Etty Bay

Tully Gorge National Park
Kareeya Power Station
White Water Rafting
Mena Creek
Falls
Mourilyan
Mourilyan Harbour
Hall Point
Feather Reef

Tully Falls
Tully Gorge State Forest Park
Downey Creek
McNamee Ck
Moresby

Koombooloomba
Japoonvale
Cowley
Double Point
Lindquist Island
Cowley Beach
Hutchison Island
Kent Island

Koombooloomba Dam
Mt Marquette •
Silkwood
Inarlinga
Kurrimine National Park
Stephens Island
Adelaide Reef

El-Arish
Maria Ck Nat Pk
Murdering Point
Kurrimine

WARNING
Never swim in waterways where this sign appears. Estuarine (saltwater) crocodiles are very dangerous.

'Tully River Station'
Alligators Nest
Feluga
Garners Beach
Bingil Bay
Clump Mountain National Park

Mt Tyson
TULLY
Sugar Mill Tours
Lacey Creek State Forest Park
Clump Point
Mission Beach
Resort

Licuala State Forest Park
Wongaling Beach

Silky Oak
Hull River Nat Pk
South Mission Beach
Resort
Mt Kootaloo
Dunk Island
Dunk Island National Park

Eurano
Lower Tully
Kennedy Track
Beaver Reef

'King Ranch'
Murrigal
River
Hull Heads
Tully Heads
Resort
Bedarra Island (Richards)

'Kirrama'
Murray Falls
Murray Falls State Forest Park
Bilyana
Family Islands

to Blencoe Falls (5km)
ROCKINGHAM BAY
WARNING
In summer, swimming may be dangerous because of box jellyfish in coastal waters. Seek medical aid if stung.

Edmund Kennedy National Park
Goold Island National Park
Brook Islands

Kennedy
Ellerbeck
Goold Island
Macushla Bay
Resort
Cape Richards
Shepherd Bay

CARDWELL
Forest Drive
Scraggy Point
Missionary Bay
Cape Sandwich

Lumholtz National Park
HERBERT
Five Mile
Hinchinbrook Channel
Ramsay Bay

Lumholtz National Park
Dalrymple Gap
Hinchinbrook Island
Nina Bay
Hinchinbrook National Park

Abergowrie
Mt Bowen •
Zoe Bay

Lumholtz National Park
Rungoo
Nina Palms Nat Pk
Hillcock Point

Wallaman Falls
Highest single-drop falls in Australia 279 metres
Broadwater S.F.P.
Mulligan Bay
George Point

Stony River
RIVER
Long Pocket
Nina Palms Nat Pk
Lucinda Point
Lucinda

Trebonne
Macknade
HALIFAX
Cordelia

Legend	
▨	National Park
▨	World Heritage Area
▨	National Park in World Heritage Area
▨	Aboriginal Land
▨	Aboriginal Land in World Heritage Area
▨	Urban Area
●	Major town
•	Town
•	Point of interest
✈	International airport
✈	Airport
━	Highway
—	Road (sealed)
– – –	Road (unsealed)
– – –	Track (4 wheel drive only)
-----	Walking trail
┼┼┼	Railway
-----	Boat route

0   5   10   15   20 kms

HULL RIVER NATIONAL PARK

 Department of Environment
PO Box 89
MISSION BEACH QLD 4852

South of Mission Beach is a small, 1250 hectare national park at the mouth of the Hull River. Its habitats are similar to those at Edmund Kennedy National Park. Access is either by boat along the Hull River, or by the 7-km Kennedy Track, which starts at the South Mission Beach jetty. The track affords a comfortable walk along beaches, rocky points and a mixture of rainforest and paperbark/eucalypt forests. There are wonderful views across to Dunk and other islands.

The most prominent rocky headland is called Tam O'Shanter Point, named after the vessel that brought Edmund Kennedy from Sydney.

TAM O'SHANTER STATE FOREST

This large State Forest extends from near the township of Silky Oak on the Bruce Highway, eastwards to Bingil Bay, but excludes the coastal strip around Mission Beach. The lowland forests grow mostly on clayey, swampy soils which support only limited areas and types of rainforest. Large areas of the rainforests are Fan Palm swamps. The palms, and other rainforest trees growing among them, supply the fruit on which cassowaries live. The Mission Beach region supports the largest remaining population of these tall, flightless birds. There are two special reserves within the State Forest.

Licuala State Forest Park

 Department of Natural Resources
PO Box 312
CARDWELL QLD 4849

Licuala is the scientific name for the Fan Palm. This majestic tree grows here in stands so closely spaced together that only a few other kinds of trees can grow among them.

There is a system of walking tracks and boardwalks that winds through this forest. A 4.6-km track connects this Park with Lacey Creek. The walk crosses several other creeks. A short side track leads to Luff Hill where there are views along the coast.

Lacey Creek State Forest Park

   Department of Natural Resources
PO Box 312
CARDWELL QLD 4849

The habitat in this small park is similar to that at Licuala Park. There is a 1-km circuit track which crosses a small creek. Certain rainforest trees along the track are identified and their importance to the cassowary explained.

ISLAND NATIONAL PARKS

There are numerous island national parks along the entire wet tropics coast from Orpheus Island, off Ingham in the south, to the Hope Islands between Bloomfield and Cooktown in the north. In many of these small parks, self-contained camping is allowed. The islands, however, have no facilities and no walking tracks. A permit is required to camp on them and fees are charged. As the islands are small, the number of campers and the lengths of stays are limited. Access is by boat only, and you need to take water and a fuel stove. Beware of marine stingers between November and May.

There are two large island national parks. One, the spectacular Hinchinbrook Island, has already been mentioned. The other is Dunk Island off Mission Beach.

« Fan Palm in Licuala State Forest Park

Dunk Island National Park

 Department of Environment
PO Box 89
MISSION BEACH QLD 4852

Most of the island not occupied by the resort and airstrip is clothed in lowland rainforest. Growing on poor soils, and in a comparatively dry area, the forest here is of a less complex type. Here and there, on exposed ridges and points, eucalypt forest dominates. Casuarina trees fringe the beaches. Sea and shore birds meet those of the rainforest along the forest edge. Numerous species of butterflies sparkle in the undergrowth. Mount Kotaloo rises to a 271 m summit which is the highest point on the island. Rocks, beaches and forests can be reached by a 13-km long network of walking tracks.

CLUMP MOUNTAIN NATIONAL PARK

 Department of Environment
PO Box 89
MISSION BEACH QLD 4852

This small, 300 hectare park protects one of the very few remaining patches of the most complex rainforests of the wet tropics — one that grows in the lowlands in places with good soil and high, year-round rainfall. Only 8 hectares of this particular forest type survive here. Exposure to cyclones blasting in from the coral sea make this patch vulnerable. Nonetheless, the tiny remnant exhibits all the characteristics of complex lowland rainforest — epiphytic ferns, orchids and mosses, large-leafed trees, vines and shrubs, buttressed trees and so on.

A 3.9-km graded walk leads to the summit of Bicton Hill. Prominent trees along this self-guiding trail are labelled and identified. Several lookouts give grand views of the forests and coastline.

Male Purple-crowned Pigeon

Fan Palm »

SECTION THREE: INNISFAIL TO CAIRNS

WOOROONOORAN NATIONAL PARK

Each reserve in the wet tropics, no matter what its size, protects a unique set of habitats and is, therefore, of vital importance. However, there are three national parks which are in the "great" category. Their greatness does not so much lie in their size, though this is substantial, but in the landforms, plants and animal associations they contain. One of these three is the remarkable Hinchinbrook Island, a self-contained wilderness of exceptional beauty. The other two, Wooroonooran National Park and Daintree National Park, as well as being spectacular, have a further significance that cannot be overstated. These are the places where rainforests have grown and flourished for as long as they have existed. Of the two, Wooroonooran is the greatest of all; it is the very core of Australia's tropical rainforest.

Wooroonooran's National Park is 79 500 hectares in area. It has as its centre-piece the twin granite mountain complex of Bartle Frere–Bellenden Ker, the highest mountains in northern Australia. It contains the last viable remnants of Australia's most complex rainforests growing in the lowlands at Downey and McNamee Creeks. In fact, this park contains nearly all the rainforest types: from those of lowlands to those on the highest mountains, and from those growing on granite soils to those growing on basalt soils. This mountain complex has the highest recorded rainfall in Australia. The tiny settlement of Topaz on the Atherton Tableland, which is surrounded by the park's forests, has the highest rainfall of any town, village or hamlet in the country. There are cyclone-ravaged rainforests on the eastern slopes and sheltered ones with gigantic trees on the western slopes.

The Mulgrave, Russell and North Johnstone Rivers rise in the park, and in their journey to the sea rush over waterfalls in spectacular, deeply-cut gorges. Walking tracks, from graded and easy to ungraded and challenging, traverse various sections of the Park.

Palmerston Section

 Department of Environment
PO Box 800
INNISFAIL QLD 4860

The Palmerston Highway follows a rainforest spur between the North and South Johnstone Rivers, through Wooroonooran National Park, as it ascends the Atherton Tableland.

Walking tracks enter the rainforest at several points along the Highway. They lead through largely unlogged forests, to rugged ravines in basalt rock with a series of exquisite waterfalls. White-water rafting can be enjoyed on the North Johnstone River below Crawford's Lookout.

Josephiné Falls

 Department of Environment
PO Box 93
MIRIWINNI QLD 4871

An easy 800-m walk through lowland rainforest takes you to Josephine Creek. Fed by Australia's highest rainfall, it is nearly always a powerful broad stream. Sometimes it is a raging torrent of white water. At Josephine Falls the Creek surges down a granite rock bar worn smooth by the water. Below the falls the water runs through an expanse of boulders and into a series of broad clear pools.

Goldfields Trail

 Department of Environment
PO Box 93
MIRIWINNI QLD 4871

The trail runs from the Boulders, near Babinda, to the Goldsborough State Forest. It is a long, but comfortable 19 km-walk through lowland rainforest over the saddle between Mounts Bartle Frere and Bellenden Ker. The area has been logged and the walk follows a gold prospecting trail of the 1930s.

« Close-up of the wing of a Rainbow Lorikeet

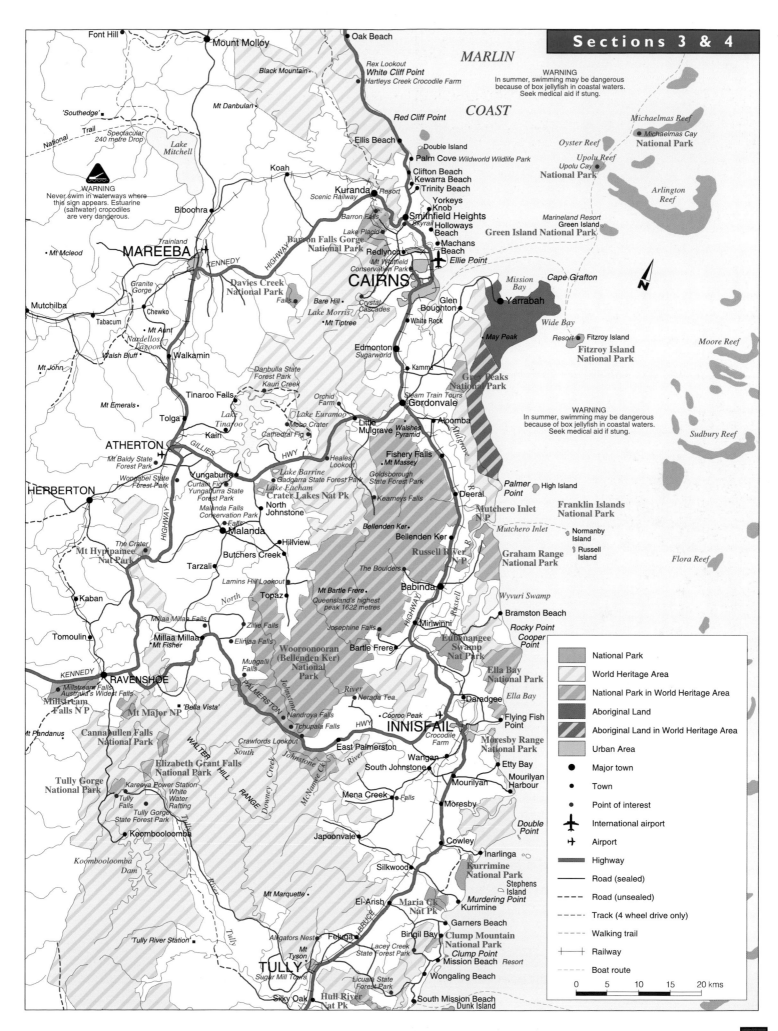

Font Hill
Mount Molloy
Oak Beach
MARLIN

Rex Lookout
White Cliff Point
Black Mountain
Hartleys Creek Crocodile Farm

WARNING
In summer, swimming may be dangerous
because of box jellyfish in coastal waters.
Seek medical aid if stung.

Mt Danbulan
Red Cliff Point
COAST

Michaelmas Reef
'Southedge'
National Trail
Michaelmas Cay
National Park

Spectacular
240 metre Drop
Lake Mitchell
Ellis Beach
Double Island
Palm Cove *Wildworld Wildlife Park*
Clifton Beach

Oyster Reef
Upolu Reef
Upolu Cay
National Park

Koah
Kewarra Beach
Trinity Beach

WARNING
Never swim in waterways where
this sign appears. Estuarine
(saltwater) crocodiles
are very dangerous.
Kuranda
Scenic Railway
Resort
Yorkeys
Knob
Smithfield Heights
Skyrail Holloways
Beach

*Arlington
Reef*

Biboohra
Barron Falls
Lake Placid
Machans
Beach
Redlynch
Marineland Resort
Green Island
Green Island National Park

MAREEBA
Trainland
KENNEDY
HIGHWAY
Mt Whitfield
Conservation Park
Ellie Point

Mt Mcleod
Davies Creek
National Park
CAIRNS
Glen
Boughton
Cape Grafton

Mutchilba
Granite Gorge
Chewko
Falls
Bare Hill
Crystal Cascades
White Rock
Yarrabah
Mission Bay

Tabacum
Mt Aunt
Lake Morris
Mt Tiptree
Wide Bay
Resort Fitzroy Island

Nardellos Lagoon
Edmonton
Sugarworld
May Peak
Fitzroy Island
National Park
Moore Reef

Walsh Bluff
Walkamin
Mt John
Kamma
Mt Emerals

Danbulla State Forest Park
Kauri Creek
Bell Peaks
National Park
Tinaroo Falls
Orchid Farm
Steam Train Tours
Gordonvale

WARNING
In summer, swimming may be dangerous
because of box jellyfish in coastal waters.
Seek medical aid if stung.
Sudbury Reef

Tolga
Lake Tinaroo
Lake Euramoo
Little
Mulgrave
Walshes Pyramid
Aloomba

GILLIES
Kairi
Mobo Crater
Cathedral Fig
ATHERTON
Mt Baldy State Forest Park
Heales Lookout
Fishery Falls
Mt Massey
Palmer Point
High Island

Yungaburra
Curtain Fig
Yungaburra State Forest Park
Lake Barrine
Gadgarra State Forest Park
Goldsborough State Forest Park
Kearneys Falls
Deeral

HERBERTON
Wongabel State Forest Park
Lake Eacham
Crater Lakes Nat Pk
Franklin Islands
National Park

Malanda Falls Conservation Park
North
Johnstone
Bellenden Ker
Mutchero Inlet
Mutchero Inlet N P
Normanby Island

Falls
Malanda
Hillview
Bellenden Ker
Russell Island

The Crater
Butchers Creek
Russell River N P
Graham Range National Park
Flora Reef

Mt Hypipamee Nat Park
Tarzali
The Boulders
Babinda

Kaban
Lamins Hill Lookout
Topaz
Mt Bartle Frere
Queensland's highest peak 1622 metres
Wyvuri Swamp
Bramston Beach

Tomoulin
North
Millaa Millaa Falls
Zillie Falls
Josephine Falls
Miriwinni
Rocky Point
Cooper Point

Millaa Millaa
Mt Fisher
Elinjaa Falls
Bartle Frere
Eubenangee Swamp Nat Park

KENNEDY
RAVENSHOE
Mungalli Falls
Wooroonooran
(Bellenden Ker)
National Park
River
Nerada Tea
Ella Bay National Park

Millstream Falls
Australia's Widest Falls
Mt Major NP
'Bella Vista'
PALMERSTON
Johnstone
Daradgee
Ella Bay

Millstream Falls N P
Nandroya Falls
Cooroo Peak
INNISFAIL
Flying Fish
Point

Mt Pandanus
Cannabullen Falls National Park
Tchupala Falls
East Palmerston
HWY
Crocodile Farm
Moresby Range National Park

WALTER
Crawfords Lookout
South
Wangan
Etty Bay

Elizabeth Grant Falls National Park
HILL
Johnstone
River
South Johnstone
Mourilyan
Mourilyan Harbour

Tully Gorge National Park
Kareeya Power Station
White Water Rafting
Mena Creek
Falls
Moresby

Tully Falls
RANGE
McNamee Ck
Downey Creek
Double Point

Tully Gorge State Forest Park
Koombooloomba
Japoonvale
Cowley
Inarlinga

Koombooloomba Dam
Silkwood
Kurrimine National Park
Stephens Island

Tully
Mt Marquette
El-Arish
Maria Ck Nat Pk
Murdering Point

'Tully River Station'
Alligators Nest
Feluga
Garners Beach
Bingil Bay
Clump Mountain National Park

TULLY
Mt Tyson
Sugar Mill Tours
Lacey Creek State Forest Park
Clump Point
Mission Beach *Resort*

BRUCE
Licuala State Forest Park
Wongaling Beach

Silky Oak
Hull River Nat Pk
South Mission Beach
Dunk Island

Legend

	National Park
	World Heritage Area
	National Park in World Heritage Area
	Aboriginal Land
	Aboriginal Land in World Heritage Area
	Urban Area
●	Major town
●	Town
•	Point of interest
✈	International airport
✈	Airport
	Highway
	Road (sealed)
	Road (unsealed)
	Track (4 wheel drive only)
	Walking trail
	Railway
	Boat route

0   5   10   15   20 kms

Mount Bartle Frere Summit Trail

Department of Environment
PO Box 93
MIRIWINNI QLD 4871

This unformed, but marked, trail traverses the summit of Mount Bartle Frere. It runs from Josephine Falls near the coast, to Gourka Road near Lamin's Hill on the Atherton Tableland. You should only attempt this 15-km trail if you are fit and have bushwalking experience. Starting at Josephine Falls, you would travel from broadleafed lowland rainforest (on granite soils), to the stunted-looking, wind-blown, rocky forests of northern Australia's highest peak. You move from hot forests full of butterflies, to cool to cold elevations where unique, high-altitude birds live (see Part 3 for range of forest types). Even though you are walking through Australia's wettest forests, the trail crosses few streams. It is a good idea to carry water. The trail ends on the Atherton Tableland in upland forests growing on basalt soils.

THE BOULDERS SCENIC RESERVE

This small reserve, adjoining Wooroonooran National Park, is administered by the Cairns City Council. Like Josephine Falls, this is a place where a fast-flowing, mountain-fed stream, in this case Babinda Creek, races through a section of granite rock. As the reserve's name suggests, this is not a waterfall, but a collection of gigantic boulders. Walking tracks follow the creek through dense lowland rainforest.

ELLA BAY NATIONAL PARK

Department of Environment
PO Box 800
INNISFAIL QLD 4860

The rainforest-covered hills of the Seymour Range are the backbone of this park. The range rises sharply from the beach. The more gentle western slopes descend to paperbark swamps and woodlands. There are no walking tracks and road access is from the Innisfail–Flying Fish Point road or along the beach. It is a pleasant walk along the beach to the rocky promontory at Cooper Point.

EUBENANGEE SWAMP NATIONAL PARK

Department of Environment
PO Box 93
MIRIWINNI QLD 4871

This small park of 155 hectares has clayey, poorly-drained soils, and as a result, is a place of lagoons, sedge-filled marshes and paperbark swamps. Galleries of riverine rainforest line the creeks. A 1.5-km track leads to a grassy hill overlooking lagoons and marshes. Here you will find good views of wetland birds and, on a clear day, Mounts Bartle Frere and Bellenden Ker.

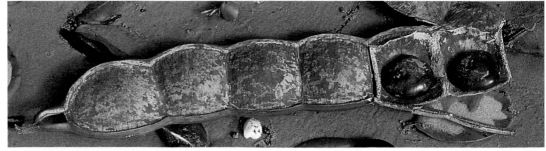

A Matchbox Bean pod washed up on the beach

« Detail of the wing of a Tailed Emperor Butterfly

RUSSELL RIVER NATIONAL PARK

 Department of Environment
PO Box 93
MIRIWINNI QLD 4871

This reserve completes Wooroonooran National Park, since its river, estuary and coastal areas are almost contiguous with the great park. It is separated from Wooroonooran by a valley that accommodates both the main north-south highway and the railway, as well as extensive fields of sugar cane. Apart from the rainforest-covered hills of the Graham Range, this park contains the usual lowland combination of rainforests, palm swamps, paperbarks and eucalypts. Extensive areas of mangroves grow along the rivers and in the estuary where the Russell and Mulgrave Rivers join. There are no facilities or walking tracks. The best way to see the mangrove forests and their varied wildlife is by a boat cruise on the estuary.

GOLDSBOROUGH VALLEY STATE FOREST

 Department of Natural Resources
PO Box 210
ATHERTON QLD 4883

This State Forest borders the Mulgrave River in the north-western edge of Wooroonooran National Park. It includes the spectacular Kearney's Falls, which is reached along an easy, graded track through complex lowland rainforest. Huge strangler fig trees, Matchbox Bean vines and scrubfowl mounds can be seen on the way. There are not many large trees, other than figs, as the forest has been logged. There is great swimming and canoeing on the river. Aborigines have had a long association with the forest. Their affinities are touched upon in a series of interpretive signs. Europeans came later to extract gold and timber and to clear the forest to grow sugar cane. The 19-km Goldfields trail runs between this Forest and The Boulders Scenic Reserve. The well-maintained camping ground is an ideal place to see butterflies and lowland birds.

MT WHITFIELD CONSERVATION PARK

 Department of Environment
PO Box 2066
CAIRNS QLD 4870

There are remnants of lowland rainforest in this small, 297 hectare reserve right on the edge of the city of Cairns. Despite its proximity to the city, the forests are rich in bird and insect life. A strenuous walk along the 7-km trail of the Blue Arrow Circuit will give you a sample of tropical rainforest as well as views of the Coral Sea coast and Cairns.

There is exciting bushwalking in many of the larger reserves.

Detail of wing of a Tailed Emperor Butterfly »

SECTION FOUR: THE ATHERTON TABLELAND

TULLY GORGE NATIONAL PARK
ELIZABETH GRANT FALLS NATIONAL PARK
CANNABULLEN FALLS NATIONAL PARK

 Department of Environment
PO Box 21
YUNGABURRA QLD 4872

 (Tully Falls only)

These three small waterfall parks are in upland rainforest on the Walter Hill Range in the catchment of the Tully River. At Tully Gorge National Park there is a short walking track through rainforest to a lookout above Tully Falls, with outstanding views of the Falls and down the Tully Gorge in the lowlands. There is no connecting road to the gorge. The waters that flow over Tully Falls have been impounded in a dam for hydro-electricity generation and the once spectacular waterfall is now a mere trickle most of the time.

Elizabeth Grant Falls and Cannabullen Falls still rush down the range in all their glory. However, there is no ready access to them and intrepid bushwalkers should contact the Department of Environment for permits and route details.

MOUNT MAJOR NATIONAL PARK

 Department of Environment
PO Box 21
YUNGABURRA QLD 4872

On the northern end of the Walter Hill Range, Mount Major's naked face of rhyolite rock rises to 1174 m. An undisturbed and unique type of cool, wet rainforest grows on the acid soils of the steep-sided mountain. There is no ready access to this park. Check with the Department of Environment for permits and route details.

MOUNT HYPIPAMEE NATIONAL PARK

 Department of Environment
PO Box 21
YUNGABURRA QLD 4872

The centre-piece of this 360 hectare park is a spectacular, sheer-sided volcanic vent, which is surrounded by a good example of upland rainforest. Mammal life is especially varied. All but one of the region's possums and the Lumholtz Tree-kangaroo live here. If you are lucky, you can see some of them at night by spotlighting. During the day, you can see many of the birds unique to the uplands and highlands, such as the Grey-headed Robin, fern wren, Atherton Scrub-wren and even, on occasions, the Golden Bowerbird.

An 800-m walking track traverses the forests and leads past streams and waterfalls to the 55-m deep volcanic crater.

Wing of a Purple-crowned Pigeon

« The volcanic vent at Mount Hypipamee

MALANDA FALLS CONSERVATION PARK

Department of Environment
PO Box 21
YUNGABURRA QLD 4872

This tiny 18.4 hectare reserve adjoins the township of Malanda, yet it is of considerable significance. The reserve's upland rainforest grows on rich basalt soils beside the North Johnstone River. It is relatively undisturbed, and has magnificent examples of walnut, black bean, tulip oak, fig and other trees. It is one of the few remaining patches of the grand forests that once covered much of the Atherton Tableland.

Two kilometres of walking track loop through the park. From the track along the river, turtles can be seen and in the mornings and evenings platypus are often observed in the pools. Many of the tree species are identified.

MOUNT BALDY STATE FOREST

Department of Natural Resources
PO Box 210
ATHERTON QLD 4883

When you stand in the town of Atherton and look west, you see a range of hills topped by rainforest. That range is part of the Great Divide, and is only a few kilometres from the centre of Atherton. You can walk up to the rainforests from the town via the rifle range, or you can drive to them in a 4-wheel drive vehicle. Drivers need a permit from the Department of Natural Resources in Atherton. The rough dirt road begins in open eucalypt woodland, which changes to upland rainforest on the higher slopes and crests of the hills. Although the forests have been heavily logged, most of the unique upland mammals and birds can be seen here. There are particularly striking examples of wet sclerophyll forest, where eucalypt forests grade into rainforest — places where gigantic Rose Gums and turpentines tower over rainforest undergrowth. At the western edge of the Great Divide the tropical rainforest ends abruptly.

WONGABEL STATE FOREST

Department of Natural Resources
PO Box 210
ATHERTON QLD 4883

Within this forest is the 2.6 km long Botanical Walk. Along this walk 190 trees are identified in an information brochure, available from the office of the Department of Natural Resources in Atherton. The walk provides a wonderful introduction to the difficult skill of identifying rainforest trees.

Next to the State Forest stands the conical Mount Wongabel, a volcanic cinder cone. Scoria rocks, erupted during the volcanic activity, cover the ground.

YUNGABURRA STATE FOREST

Department of Natural Resources
PO Box 210
ATHERTON QLD 4883

This small remnant forest is also in a volcanic zone surrounded by cinder cones. Just as at at Wongabel, the ground here is made up of boulders of scoria. This forest has been preserved to protect a single tree — the great Yungaburra curtain fig. This strangler fig has a 15 m high "curtain" of roots cascading down its trunk. It is just one example of the imposing majesty of the tropical rainforest's great trees, and the power and architecture of living plants.

Top to bottom: A Tooth-billed Bowerbird sings at his court. This bird is unique to the region's upland rainforests; the court of a Tooth-billed Bowerbird is a cleared area on the forest floor which the bird decorates with leaves placed upside down »

GADGARRA STATE FOREST

Department of Natural Resources
PO Box 210
ATHERTON QLD 4883

At Gadgarra State Forest, just beyond Lake Eacham National Park, another great tree has been preserved — a Red Cedar. Grand examples of valuable trees, except for the commercially worthless figs, are extremely rare. The survival of this enormous Red Cedar, with its great buttresses, is therefore most remarkable. Red Cedars are deciduous and if you were to visit this tree in winter, it would be bare of leaves. The huge clumps of epiphytic ferns are then most conspicuous. The tree is perhaps at its most attractive in early spring when it grows its pinkish new leaves.

CRATER LAKES NATIONAL PARK

Department of Environment
PO Box 21
YUNGABURRA QLD 4872

The clear, pure waters of Lake Eacham and Lake Barrine are held in the craters of volcanoes. Both lakes are encircled by well-made walking tracks; the one at Barrine is 5.14 km long, while the one at Eacham is 2.8 km. Lake Barrine has a tour boat operating on the lake. The Barrine walk winds past huge figs, cedars and silky oak trees, but its botanical glory is two giant bull kauri trees growing side-by-side on the Lake's edge at the start of the trail. This species of tree is considered to be endangered.

Another of the lakes' special charms is their bays and inlets. They are often framed in loops of lianes, weeping bunches of flowering orchids, epiphytic ferns and tree branches reaching far out over the water. You may see many of the upland rainforest birds, but also moorhens, ducks, cormorants, darters and other water birds. Water dragons sunbathe on logs at the water's edge and in winter, Amethyst Pythons catch the sun while coiled low in the trees.

DANBULLA STATE FOREST

Department of Natural Resources
PO Box 210
ATHERTON QLD 4883

This is part of a great arc of State Forests that stretches from Wooroonooran National Park to the hills west of Cairns. The Danbulla State Forest runs along the eastern and northern shores of the man-made Lake Tinaroo.

The 28-km Danbulla Forest Drive winds its way mostly through rainforest, but also through eucalypt forests and softwood plantations. There are many interesting stops that are clearly marked. The Cathedral Tree is another Curtain Fig, one growing in dense forest. At Mobo Creek there are deep, mysterious-looking rainforest pools. Lake Euramoo is another crater lake, and nearby there is a short botanical walk through relatively undisturbed forest. Along the Kauri Creek walking track are large Red Cedar trees and a clear stream running over coarse white sand derived from granite rocks.

There are roads that lead into the hills, such as the one to Mount Edith, which traverses moss- and fern-draped wet forest to a lookout with views over wide expanses of rainforest. A permit to travel the hill roads is required from the office of the Department of Natural Resources in Atherton.

Along the main Forest Drive there are frequent views of Lake Tinaroo and several roads lead to camping and picnic spots on its shore.

« Close-up of a tail feather of a Channel-billed Cuckoo

BARRON GORGE NATIONAL PARK

Department of Environment
PO Box 2066
CAIRNS QLD 4870

The national park runs from the western edge of the city of Cairns, along the gorge of the Barron River and up the eastern escarpment to Kuranda. You can travel through it on foot, by car, by railway, and, over a section of it, on the Skyrail cableway. While the park's rainforests are accessible, they are not of the most complex type.

The park's original attraction was the great and wild Barron Falls on the outskirts of Kuranda. Since 1935, most of its water has been diverted for hydro-electricity generation. The falls can still be seen in full flow after days of heavy monsoon or cyclonic rain.

Rail and aerial cableway connect the lower gorge and the upper portions around Kuranda. The lower Gorge, where there are some delightful walks, can be reached by road from Cairns. For the adventurous, the historic Douglas and Smith Tracks follow the ridges either side of Stoney Creek valley to the Atherton Tableland. The train journey through the gorge — from Cairns to Kuranda — is one of the most beautiful in the country. The Skyrail gives a unique perspective on the rainforest canopy.

MACALISTER RANGE STATE FOREST

Department of Natural Resources
PO Box 210
ATHERTON QLD 4883

Between Kuranda and Mossman, a corridor of dry country separates two wet regions. The MacAlister Range runs along most of this gap. The spectacular Cook Highway is squeezed between the range and the Coral Sea.

A dirt road, accessible by 4-wheel drive only, follows the western edge of the range from Kuranda to Julatten. In places it travels through various types of the drier rainforests dominated by wattle trees and wait-a-while vines. A permit is required from the Department of Natural Resources to travel the road and to camp along it.

The Northern Snapping Turtle lives in the wet tropics' rivers and creeks.

Fruit of the Raceme Ginger »

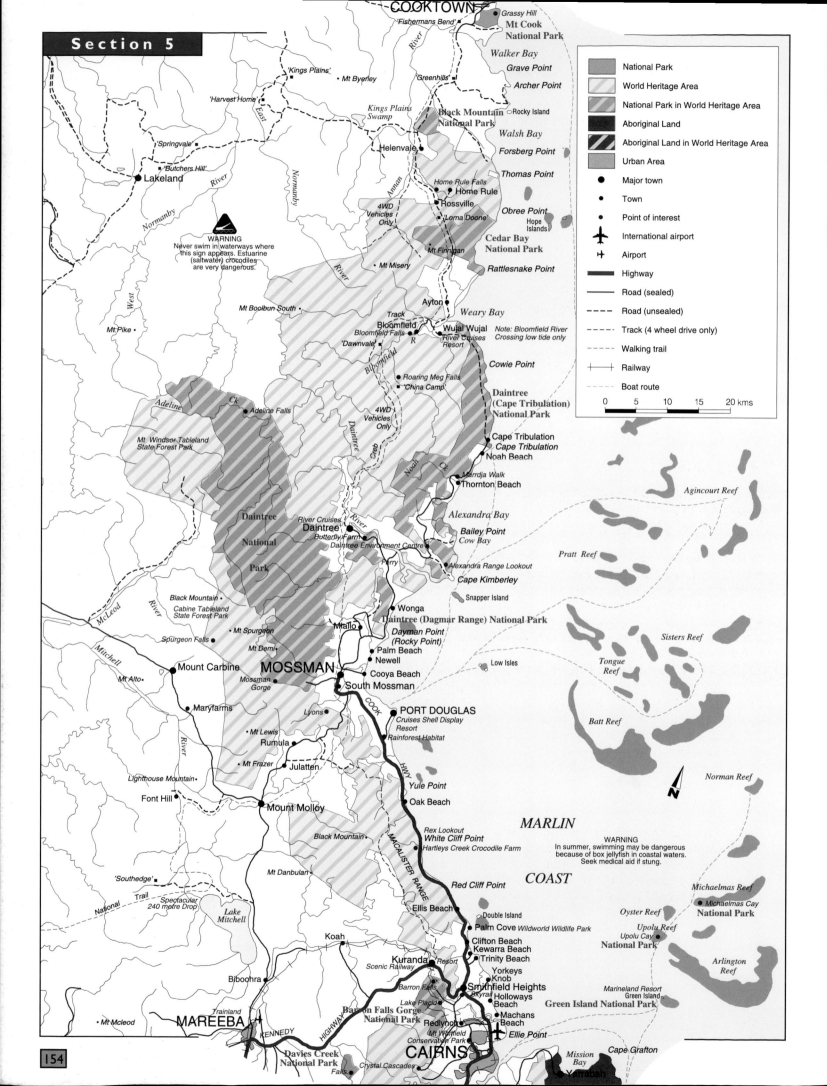

COOKTOWN

Grassy Hill
'Fishermans Bend'
Mt Cook National Park
Walker Bay
Grave Point
Archer Point
'Kings Plains'
• Mt Byerley
Greenhills
• Rocky Island
Kings Plains Swamp
Black Mountain National Park
Walsh Bay
Forsberg Point
'Harvest Home'
Helenvale
Thomas Point
'Springvale'
Lakeland
'Butchers Hill'
Home Rule Falls
• Home Rule
• Rossville
Obree Point
Hope Islands
4WD Vehicles Only
'Lorna Doone'
Cedar Bay National Park
Rattlesnake Point
• Mt Boolbun South
• Mt Misery
Mt Finnigan
Ayton
Weary Bay

WARNING
Never swim in waterways where this sign appears. Estuarine (saltwater) crocodiles are very dangerous.

• Mt Pike
Track
Bloomfield
Bloomfield Falls
'Dawnvale'
R
Wujal Wujal
River Cruises Resort
Note: Bloomfield River Crossing low tide only
Cowie Point
• Roaring Meg Falls
'China Camp'
4WD Vehicles Only
Daintree (Cape Tribulation) National Park
Adeline
Ck
• Adeline Falls
Mt Windsor Tableland State Forest Park
Cape Tribulation
Cape Tribulation
Noah Beach
Marrdja Walk
Thornton Beach
Alexandra Bay
Daintree
River Cruises
Daintree
Butterfly Farm
Daintree Environment Centre
Perry
Bailey Point
Cow Bay
Alexandra Range Lookout
National
Cape Kimberley
Snapper Island
Park
Black Mountain
Cabine Tableland State Forest Park
• Mt Spurgeon
Wonga
Daintree (Dagmar Range) National Park
Spurgeon Falls
Mt Demi
Miallo
Dayman Point (Rocky Point)
• Mt Alto
Mount Carbine
Mossman Gorge
MOSSMAN
Palm Beach
Newell
Low Isles
Cooya Beach
• Maryfarms
Lyons
South Mossman
PORT DOUGLAS
Cruises Shell Display Resort
Rainforest Habitat
• Mt Lewis
Rumula
• Mt Frazer
Julatten
Lighthouse Mountain •
Yule Point
Font Hill
Oak Beach
Mount Molloy
MARLIN
Rex Lookout
Black Mountain
White Cliff Point
Hartleys Creek Crocodile Farm
WARNING
In summer, swimming may be dangerous because of box jellyfish in coastal waters. Seek medical aid if stung.
Mt Danbulan
COAST
'Southedge'
Red Cliff Point
National Trail
Spectacular 240 metre Drop
Lake Mitchell
Ellis Beach
Double Island
Palm Cove Wildworld Wildlife Park
Koah
Clifton Beach
Kewarra Beach
Kuranda Resort
Trinity Beach
Scenic Railway
Yorkeys Knob
Biboohra
Smithfield Heights
Holloways Beach
Barron Falls
Skyrail
Green Island National Park
Lake Placid
Machans Beach
Trainland
MAREEBA
Barron Falls Gorge National Park
Redlynch
Ellie Point
• Mt Mcleod
Mt Whitfield Conservation Park
CAIRNS
KENNEDY
Davies Creek National Park
Crystal Cascades
Falls
Mission Bay
Cape Grafton
Yarrabah

Agincourt Reef

Pratt Reef

Sisters Reef

Tongue Reef

Batt Reef

Norman Reef

Michaelmas Reef
• Michaelmas Cay
National Park
Oyster Reef
Upolu Reef
Upolu Cay
National Park
Arlington Reef
Marineland Resort
Green Island

Legend

	National Park
	World Heritage Area
	National Park in World Heritage Area
	Aboriginal Land
	Aboriginal Land in World Heritage Area
	Urban Area
●	Major town
•	Town
·	Point of interest
✈	International airport
✈	Airport
━━	Highway
───	Road (sealed)
-----	Road (unsealed)
-- --	Track (4 wheel drive only)
‧‧‧‧	Walking trail
┼─┼─	Railway
- - -	Boat route

0   5   10   15   20 kms

DAINTREE NATIONAL PARK

Daintree National Park is the umbrella name for four separate parks which do not actually join together: Mossman Gorge, two sections of the Dagmar Range and a narrow strip along the coast between the Daintree and Bloomfield Rivers. All sections together cover nearly 76 000 hectares of some of the wet tropics' most important rainforests. They constitute the third great rainforest national park.

Mossman Gorge

 Department of Environment
PO Box 251
MOSSMAN QLD 4873

At 56 500 hectares in area, this is the largest portion of the park. It is readily accessible only at Mossman Gorge itself. Here, the Mossman River tumbles out of the hills and flows strongly among giant granite boulders. There are many wide, clear rock pools with native freshwater fishes of many species. The constant moisture from the river's spray, as it races between the rocks, makes for hanging gardens of epiphytes, from mosses and lichens, to ferns and orchids, on the riverside trees. A 2.7-km circuit track loops through wonderful examples of lowland forest growing on granite soils. Only fit and experienced bushwalkers should venture into the upland wilderness beyond the gorge and a permit from the Department of Environment is required. It is a region of rugged scarps, deep river valleys, clear mountain streams, rapids and waterfalls, and pristine upland rainforest.

Cape Tribulation

 Department of Environment
PO Box 251
MOSSMAN QLD 4873

Once you cross the Daintree River on the vehicular ferry, you enter one of the most magical parts of the tropical rainforest. Some of the wet tropics' highest mountains, such as Thornton Peak and Mount Hemmant, with their summits more often than not swathed in mist and clouds, have slopes covered in rainforest that sweep down to sandy beaches. Crystal-clear creeks cascade down the gullies and enter the sea through a maze of mangroves. These mountains are among the wettest places in Australia — possibility as wet as Bartle Frere–Bellenden Ker. However, no rain gauges have ever been placed on the northern mountains so no exact figures are available.

The coastal stretch of forest is the largest area of lowland rainforest remaining and is, therefore, of great significance. Most important of all, many primitive plants that give evidence of the great age of these forests are still found here. Unfortunately only a few short walking tracks allow you to explore these wonders. There are no trails up any of the mountains.

At Alexandra Lookout there are extensive views of many habitats, including the Daintree River meandering through mangrove forests to the sea.

The Marrdja Boardwalk at Oliver Creek offers a wonderful introduction to the lowland rainforest. The 800-m track ends at a boardwalk through mangrove forest at the mouth of the creek.

At Cape Tribulation itself there are more short walks giving exciting views of the coast and mountains.

Cape Tribulation and Mount Sorrow were named by Captain James Cook as he sailed along this coast in 1770. The names do not reflect his views of these magnificent forests, but rather his feelings at his ship being severely damaged on a nearby reef.

The road beyond Cape Tribulation to the Bloomfield River is steep and rough, with many bouldery creek crossings. It is suitable for high-clearance, 4-wheel drive vehicles only.

Fallen flower of a Beach Barringtonia »

CARBINE TABLELAND AND MOUNT WINDSOR TABLELAND STATE FORESTS

 Department of Natural Resources
PO Box 210
ATHERTON QLD 4883

These rugged and isolated plateaus on the Great Dividing Range are exceptional wilderness areas. A narrow saddle connects the two tablelands, which have extensive summit areas (over 1100 m) covered with rainforest. These were completely undisturbed until logging began in the 1970s. Plant and animal life is typical of mountain areas. The other species of tree-kangaroo — the Bennett's Tree-kangaroo — is occasionally seen here.

Access is by 4-wheel drive vehicle only and a permit is required from the Department of Natural Resources.

CEDAR BAY NATIONAL PARK

 Department of Environment
PO Box 611
COOKTOWN QLD 4871

Cedar Bay gained a degree of notoriety in the 1970s when squatters, seeking a different way of life, were evicted from the park. Cedar Bay's complex rainforests from lowland to mountain are the northernmost full-blown tropical rainforests of the wet tropics. Gap Creek, with its calm, clear pools full of native fish separates the lowlands to the east, from the upland forests to the west which culminate in the mountain forests of Mount Finnigan).

There are no formal walking tracks or other facilities. However, several well-worn bush tracks lead from the Bloomfield road to the coast. The 7-hour walk from Home Rule to the northern end of Cedar Bay includes lowland rainforest and great coastal scenery.

BLACK MOUNTAIN NATIONAL PARK

 Department of Environment
PO Box 611
COOKTOWN QLD 4871

At these spectacular and gigantic piles of granite boulders, the World Heritage tropical rainforests come to an end. The place is too dry to support extensive or complex rainforest; it persists only along streams and gullies. There are no walking tracks onto or around these hills. Should you walk about, beware of stinging trees. Do not underestimate the size of the boulders or the extent of the hills. It is easy to become disoriented and lose your way.

The chowchilla's clear, far-carrying voice is characteristic of the tropical rainforests.

« *Top to bottom:* The Daintree River Ringtail Possum; fruit of Grey Bollywood; Noisy Pitta

INDEX

Detail of the wing of a Forest Kingfisher »

« A new leaf of an Atherton Oak

First published by Steve Parish Publishing Pty Ltd, 1999
PO Box 1058, Archerfield BC, Queensland 4108, Australia

© copyright Stanley Breeden, 1999

ISBN: 1 876282 11 8

Maps supplied by MAPgraphics
Designed by Leanne Nobilio, Steve Parish Publishing
Edited by Rod Ritchie and Julia Walkden
Printed in Hong Kong by South China Printing
Film separations by Inprint Pty Ltd, Brisbane, Queensland